PLUS+

Edited
by
Bethany
Rutter

PLUS+

Style
inspiration
for
everyone

Foreword
by
Nicolette
Mason

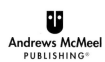

Andrews McMeel
PUBLISHING®

Andrews McMeel Publishing
a division of Andrews McMeel Universal
1130 Walnut Street, Kansas City, Missouri 64106

www.andrewsmcmeel.com

First published by Ebury Publishing in 2018.
www.eburypublishing.co.uk

19 20 21 22 23 TEN 10 9 8 7 6 5 4 3 2 1

ISBN: 978-1-4494-9357-8

Library of Congress Control Number: 2018951478

Editor: Allison Adler
Art Director/Designer: Julie Barnes
Production Editor: Dave Shaw
Production Manager: Tamara Haus

ATTENTION: SCHOOLS AND BUSINESSES

Andrews McMeel books are available at quantity discounts with
bulk purchase for educational, business, or sales promotional use.
For information, please e-mail the Andrews McMeel Publishing
Special Sales Department: specialsales@amuniversal.com.

For every fat babe who
ever inspired me.

Foreword by Nicolette Mason

I'd love to pretend that I came out of the womb as this body positive, self-loving, confidently fat individual, but like most people who live in "othered" bodies, I was a self-conscious, self-doubting, chubby Middle Eastern girl who really wanted to be pretty. I was probably only 7-years-old when I became conscious of the fact that there was something "wrong" with the way I looked. I was desperate to fit into the mainstream norm of fashion and beauty, and so badly wanted to be cool, a universal feeling that felt even more exaggerated growing up in image-conscious LA. I spent my childhood and adolescence wanting to be thin, and literally squeezed my zaftig body into too-tight clothes just to play along.

When I was 16, my desperation took me to an ultra-posh boutique in Beverly Hills that had become *the* fashion destination among young Hollywood. I scanned the store for jersey and stretchy seams and little hints that something might fit, and zeroed in on a pair of sleek, faded jeans with a nary-in-sight elastic waistband. I clutched them and ran to the fitting room: These jeans were my ticket to being inducted into fashion's exclusive club. I called my mom over, feeling so proud and confident, knowing how much she'd love them too, only to be greeted by a hearty, belly-deep laugh. "What? Don't they look good?" I implored, while turning around and showing them off. My mom kept laughing, and motioned for one of the sales girls to come look at me peacocking in the jeans. "They're maternity jeans," she giggled. "Please, tell her they're maternity jeans!" The sales girl stood awkwardly, until she burst and joined my mom's chorus of amusement. I scurried back into the fitting room, peeled off the jeans, and ran out of the boutique without looking up.

Even though I felt rejected by fashion, I was still obsessed with it; it wasn't just the maternity jeans incident — it was constant micro-aggressions and the absence of anyone like me gracing the glossies. The pages of *Vogue* were plastered on my walls, and I fawned over Marc Jacobs and Anna Sui, fantasizing about what a perfect, designer-clad life might look like in a size 6 body. There was no Beth Ditto or Lizzo or Ashley Graham to serve as my fashion template. Whenever there was a body that looked like mine, it was understood — whether blatantly said or through coded language — that fatness was inherently bad. Fat was synonymous with ugliness, and if fashion was a world curated by aesthetics, which defined beauty, there was no way fat and fashion could coexist.

Even though I spent my entire life feeling hyper aware of my body and the space I took up, it took me years to self-identify as plus size, and even longer to find power in that identity. I was trained to shrink and obscure my frame, to disguise my shape and size through black, drapey clothing, and make myself as invisible as possible. Stripes? Not for me. Wearing white? It would only exaggerate my size. Patterns? Why would I want to draw even more attention to my ample ass? There were so many rules, all of them reinforcing the idea that fashion was not a world in which I was allowed to participate.

And yet, I found my way in. I was first introduced to body positivity in online Fatshion communities. That lead to creating my own blog, and then being invited to write for *Vogue Italia*, and then being a contributing editor at *Marie Claire*, and then creating collections for brands like ModCloth and Addition Elle, and then starring in international campaigns. There are so many "and then's," and that journey lead me to this utterly transformative moment when I joined forces with my friend and fashion pioneer Gabi Gregg to create our own plus-size brand, Premme. It's a path that only became possible thanks to the labor of many people, especially women of color and queer femmes — who created a language and vocabulary for body positivity, and acted as thought leaders and creators of our own empowering fashion. While we may not have been invited to the mainstream fashion table, there's something to be said for having to create our own damn party; it's kind of a revolutionary act to adorn and dress ourselves, to look in the mirror and say, "Damn, I look good," without an invitation from the establishment.

I could never have anticipated that fashion would finally reach a tipping point where it was understood, and even celebrated, that beauty exists outside the margins of the thin, white, eurocentric ideal. I only ever dreamed that diversity would become the standard — and not just in a tokenizing way — that truly reflected our world of different ethnicities, sizes and shapes, of different levels of ability, of an entire spectrum of gender identities and sexualities. It's a world where those same *Vogue*-approved designers, like Christian Siriano and Prabal Gurung and Clements Ribeiro, are making clothes for us. And where our models, our Ashley Grahams and Tess Hollidays and Candice Huffines and Precious Lees, are getting their own covers. To be part of a culture that is creating fashion and media for us, that is chipping away at the archaic ideal of beauty standards and style one hashtag at a time, is a literal dream come true.

I'm so excited and proud of Bethany for creating this book, a physical book, and giving us a space to revel in our beauty, our visibility and our really damn good style. The power of visibility of seeing a mirror of ourselves reflected back to us, cannot be underestimated. It is in those mirrors where we can find our identities, our truths and our beauty. And if the world of fashion is still new and scary and feels unapproachable, please let this book act as the starting point — and find us, join us and be your glorious, fat, fashionable self.

PLUS +

Introduction by Bethany Rutter

We've come a long way, baby.

While I'm under no impression that things are actively good or easy for plus-size women out there in the big bad world, our fashion universe has expanded more than I could possibly have imagined when I first started shopping for plus sizes. The amount of choice we're presented with today is just astronomical by comparison, but still a fraction of what's available for women who aren't plus size. This means we exist in a sweet spot: access to genuinely excellent fashion, but the pressure to be resourceful with it — the pressure to bring out the best in what's available, the pressure to style pieces in ways that reflect our personalities because the pieces themselves aren't quite right.

The plus-size fashion landscape has changed, but it's not changing quickly enough. We've gone from a single option on the UK high street to the Internet dominating everything, offering more choice than we've ever had. Traditional retailers are still lagging behind, with tiny, cramped corners at the back of high street shops "dedicated" to a disappointing plus-size range.

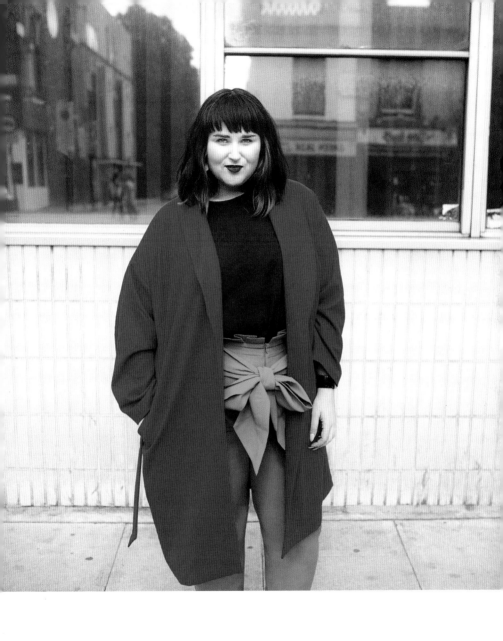

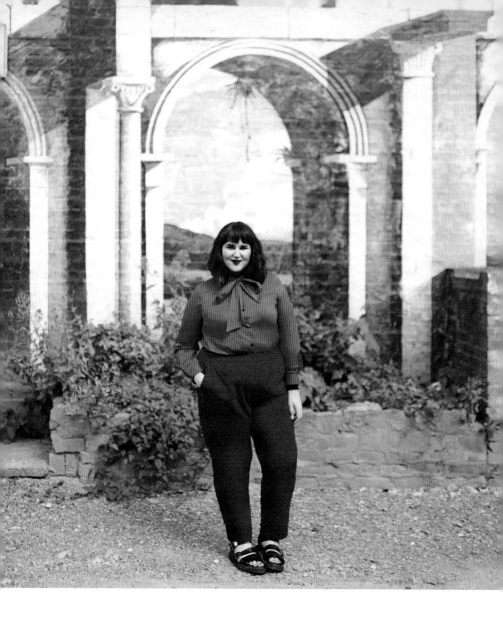

Online-only retailers like Premme, Universal Standard and Plus Equals are swooping in to rescue us with bold, decisive designs where traditional retailers are failing. When I designed my own collection with navabi (incidentally, also online-only), I was able to design into existence pieces that have *never existed before* in plus sizes. That shouldn't be possible in a booming industry that's been around for years. We shouldn't be able to invent things for the first time in our sizes when the high street produces endless iterations of trend-led items for thin women every season.

And it's people *in this book* who are changing things for the better. I believe that plus-size women on the Internet are changing the game.

I wasn't even an early adopter of plus-size fashion blogging — or *fatshion* blogging. The LiveJournal community Fatshionista existed for years before I picked up a camera and documented my outfits: Amanda Piasecki started it way back in 2004. That community was a place for fat fashion to be celebrated, as well as the bodies within the clothes. A place to document your plus-size body and what it's wearing, a place to say "I am allowed to participate in fashion. This is a space for me."

In the intervening years, the number of plus-size women representing their bodies online through traditional blogging, Instagram, YouTube and more has gone through the roof. It was partly from this extremely rich pool that I drew the contributors to this book. The word "influencer" gets thrown around a lot, but the plus-size fashion world is lucky to have people like our cover girl Gabi Gregg, as well as Nicolette Mason, Danie Vanier and loads

The plus-size fashion landscape has changed, but it's not changing quickly enough.

of others who take styling plus-size fashion to another level and who make a huge impact on what's available for us to wear and how we wear it.

One of the main reasons the online plus-size world has flourished so quickly and with such vibrancy, energy and life is that we have to be our own role models. The relative lack of plus-size role models, or even visible plus-size people — aspirational or not — in the mainstream media has given rise to a culture of plus-size women documenting ourselves on the Internet. It's a way of affirming the fact we exist. It's a way of giving ourselves a platform that is so rarely given to us by film, television, women's magazines. If we don't carry out our own representation, no one is going to do it for us. If we will never see ourselves on the cover of a magazine, it becomes all the more vital to see ourselves *somewhere*, and that somewhere has become the Internet.

Because we represent ourselves online, this representation exists in digital photos, captions, Instagram stories, fleeting moments. These things are ephemeral, and I wanted to make something permanent. I wanted to put all this on paper, to create a beautiful artifact that records the amazing work so many of us are doing.

Although I was never going to be able to include every single plus-size woman who has made an impression on me since the dawn of the Internet, I wanted to do my best for this book to reflect the many, many ways there are of being plus size, of expressing yourself within that fashion framework. It was important to me to reflect that many, if not most, of the people doing the best work in this space are black women, whether or not their efforts are always rewarded. I wanted to include women from the Global South, transgender women, Muslim women who either do or do not wear a hijab, indigenous women, queer women, women above a UK size 24, women whose first language is not English, people who don't identify as women at all. These are the people around whom this movement revolves, and I wanted to put down on paper the fact they're here, they've always been here and we need more people like them.

My intention with this book is to create a record of where we are right now. I want to document as many of the amazing plus-size outfits as I can, display the resourcefulness, the sheer style that goes into them. But I also intend this book to serve as inspiration, whether that's specific looks I've included here, new people for you to follow online (hence the usernames!) or just the feeling of calm that comes from seeing many, many photos of people with a similar body to yours, buying from a similar pool of clothes as you, that might translate to you trying something new.

So let this book be a record of how far we've come, filled with people who know we have so much further left to go and are having so much fun getting us there.

I — and other plus-size women — often complain that we always end up having to talk about and defend our bodies when we really just want to talk about clothes. It often feels as if we don't have the right to just participate in fashion. That's why I wanted the focus of this book to be on clothes, not bodies. But I knew all along that can never fully be true of plus-size fashion: Our bodies are political. How we present them is a statement. Whether we make "effort" or not, whether we're "feminine" or not, whether we manipulate the shape of our bodies or not — we're always laboring under the knowledge our bodies are different, are other, are judged more harshly than thin bodies. Through trying to curate a book about clothes, I realized it will always, always, be about bodies.

So let this book be a record of how far we've come, filled with people who know we have so much further left to go and are having so much fun getting us there. A testament to our creativity, a testament to the sheer diversity of the plus-size world, a way for you to get to know your next plus-size style crush, a place to get inspiration for your next outfit, a celebration of what we already have and a loud scream for more.

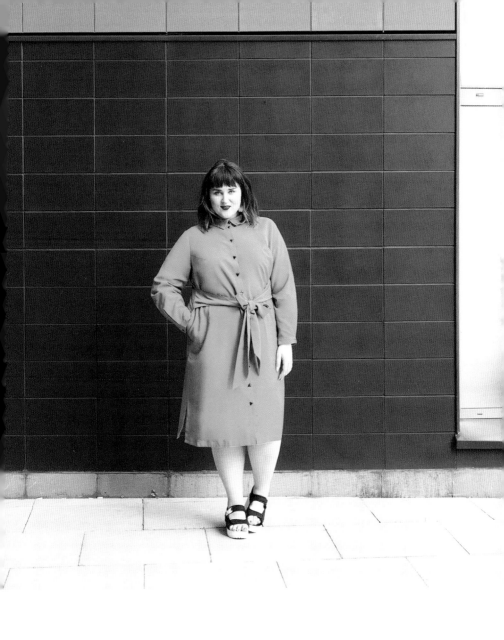

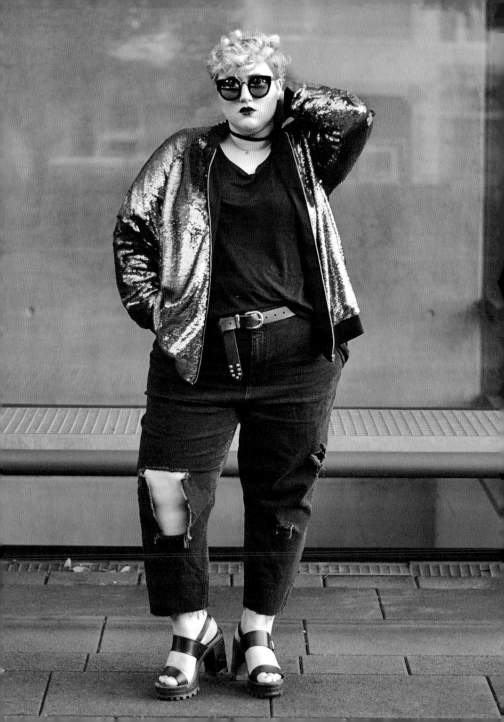

Isabell Decker
@DressingOutsideTheBox

Due to working in the fashion industry I have always been drawn to the latest fashion trends. I never wanted to let the fact of being fat and having limited fashion resources affect my style and personal expression. I guess that has helped me to form a style which I would describe as contemporary and sophisticated combined with my fondness for androgynous styling and tailoring.

Musemo Handahu
@MissLionHunter

My style is unafraid! Period.

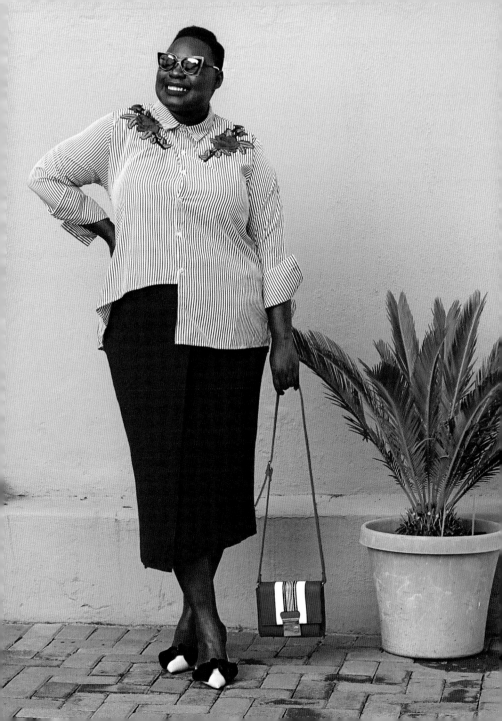

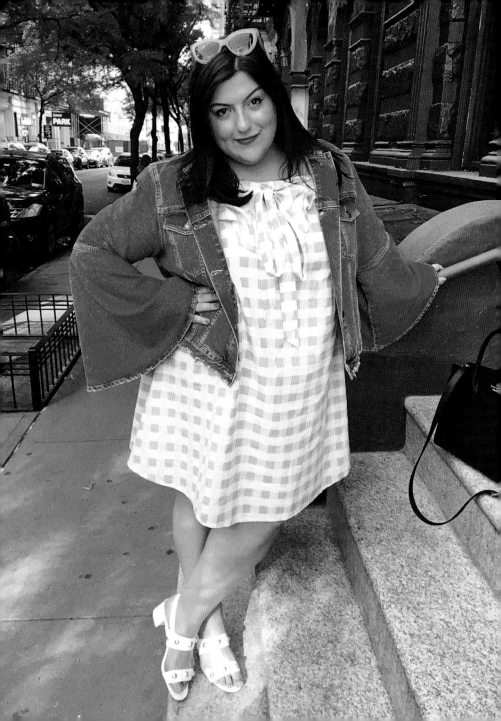

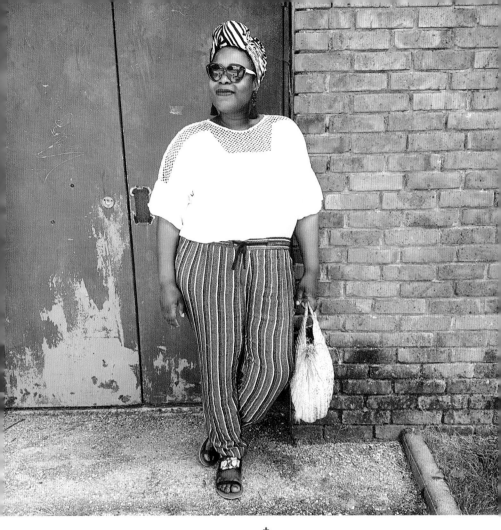

Danielle Ahanda @BestofD

Honor my curves.

Stella Boonshoft @StellaBoonshoft

I'm super inspired by silhouettes of the 1960s and '70s. I used to hate my body and try to hide myself with more masculine styles, but these days shift dresses, bright prints, and dramatic sleeves are my uniform. Fashion should make you feel like yourself — and when I'm all femmed out and showing a little leg — I feel like me.

Adwoa Darko
@auntyadj

I fluctuate between bright dresses to sports luxe, but always add a Ghanaian flair. I accessorize with headwraps, oversized rings and big necklaces. I love to accentuate my waist and cleavage, wear way too much mesh and my shoes are always impractical.

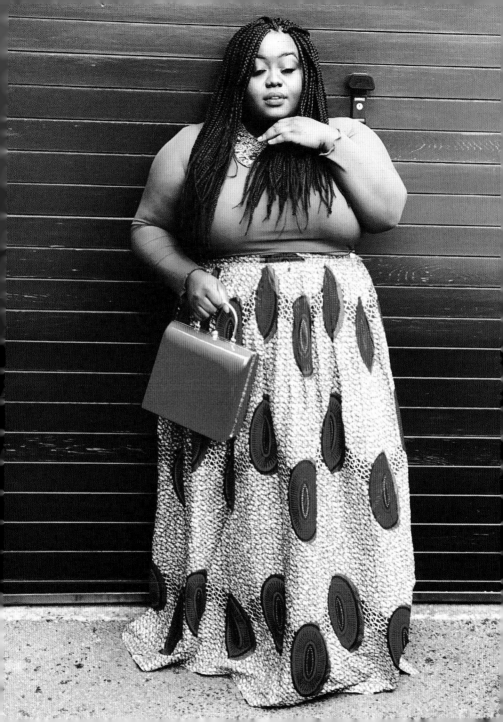

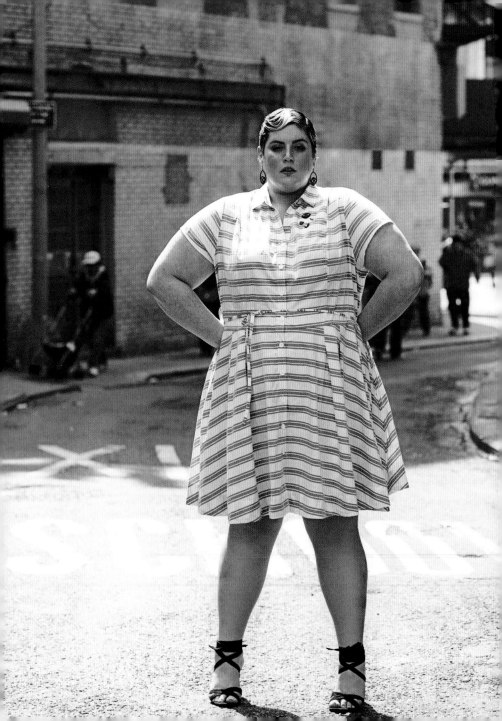

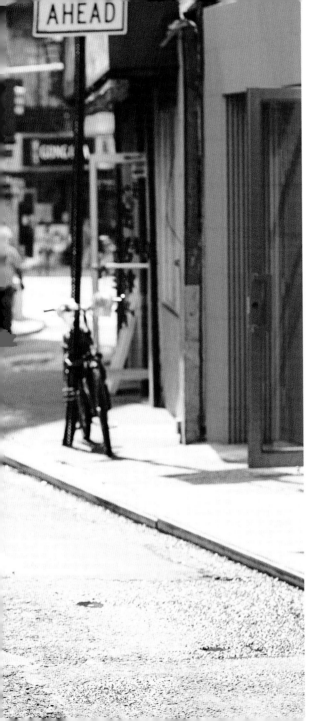

Shay Neary
@WatchShaySlay

Style is defining the clothes you're wearing. My style changes day to day as I'm a style chameleon. My mood often dictates my style. I can go from bohemian-casual realness, to quirky-retro chic, then there's the occasional urban-nightlife Amazonian, and last but not least the girl-next-door entrepreneur.

Photographer:
Lydia Hudgens

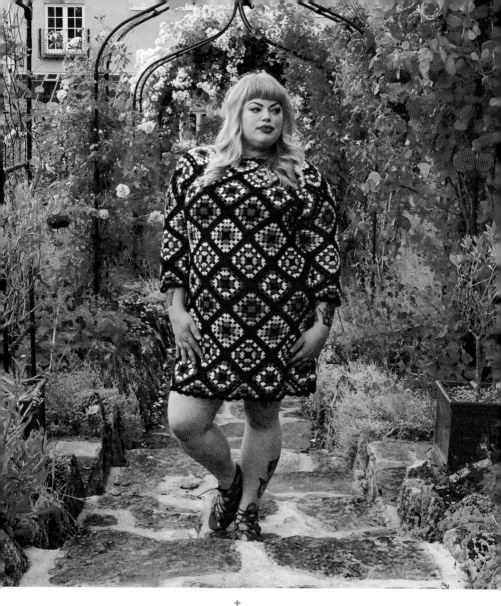

Sam Rowswell @FattyBoomTatty

My style varies depending on my mood but what never changes is my love of forgotten fabrics. I'm drawn to old, shiny polyester, mesh, pleats and velvet. Whether it's the entire garment or added touches, I love how my wardrobe can evoke childhood memories.

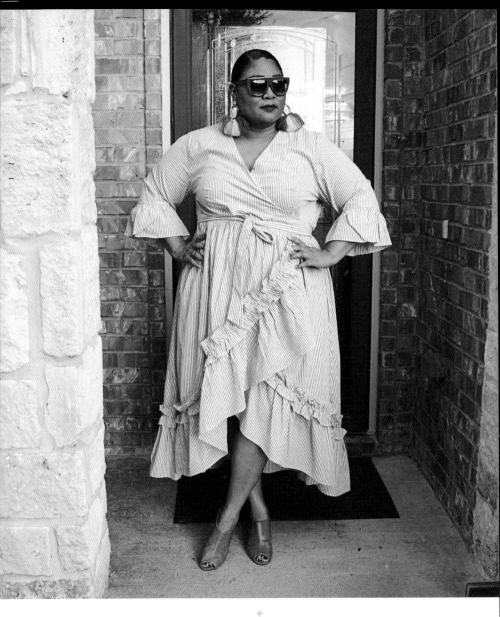

Kiah Torres @RezToTheCity

*If I had to categorize my style, I would call it classically
chic with a touch of glam/drama.*

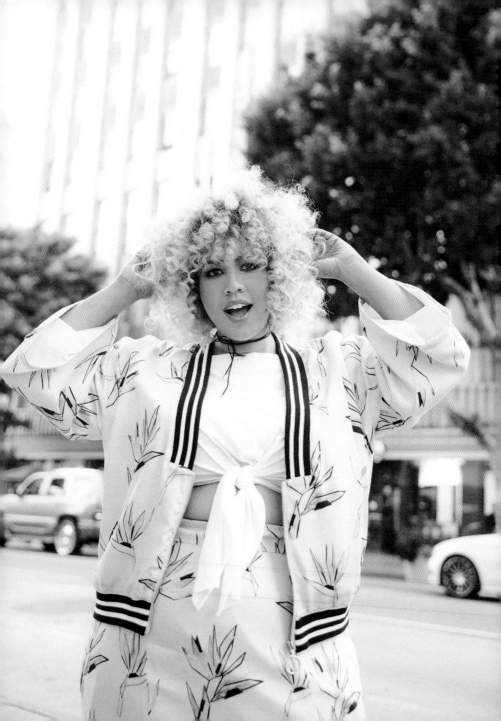

Gabi Gregg
@Gabifresh

I reject the idea that we should fill our closet with timeless classic pieces — I mean, yes, for sure I have a great pair of skinny jeans and a little black dress, but I love to look back on outfits and remember the trends of the time. Fashion should be about having fun, not making sure our outfits will age well!

Emilie Darel
@Les_Coquetteries_Demilie

*Being plus size doesn't stop me
from having my style. I love
having original looks that are
chic and trend-based. I feel good
in my body and in my clothes.*

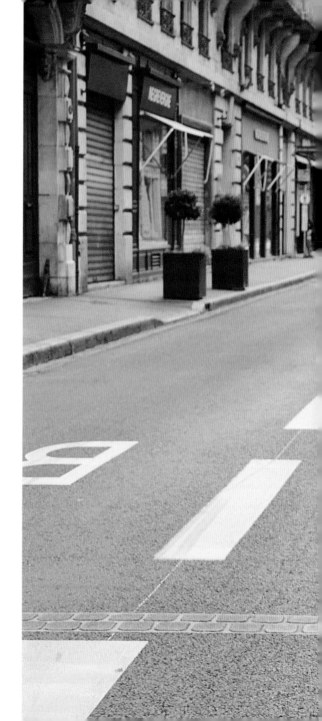

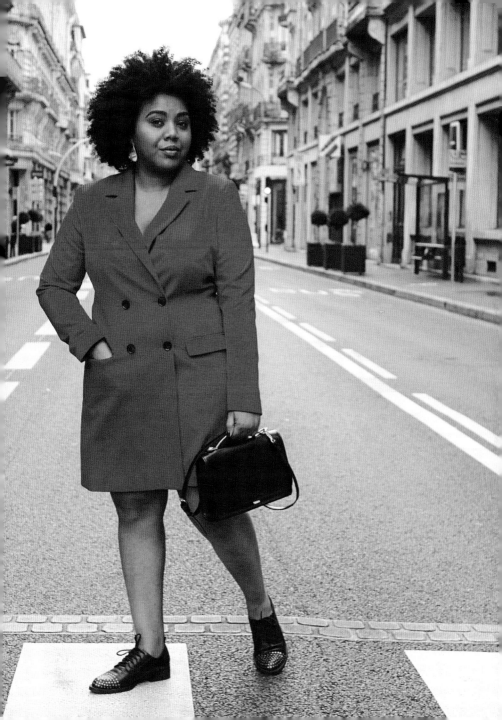

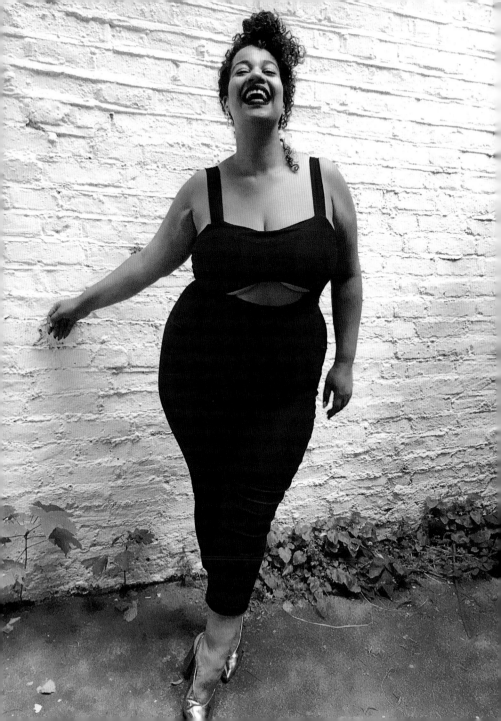

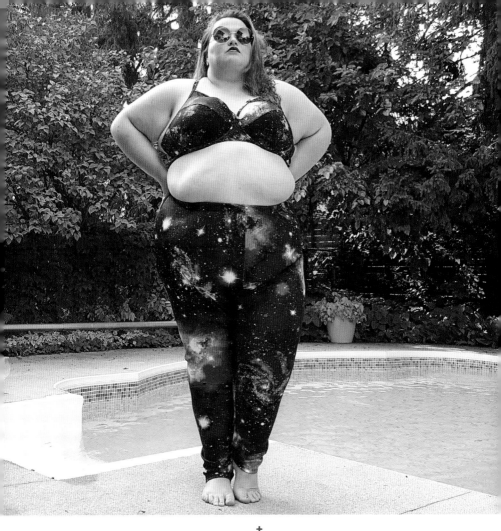

+

Rebecca Northcott @BeccaBexBest

*I am a big believer in wearing what you want to express how you feel, I wear colors/
prints that are both bold and have a colorful/vibrant palette. It's not always in fashion
but it makes me excited to start my day, get out and live my life. I was titled vivacious by
a friend and I think that sums me up perfectly with my style.*

+

Olivia Campbell @CurvyCampbell

*My style is minimal yet flamboyant. Fashion for me is a way to show off the many
facets of my personality, as well as my phenomenal cleavage!*

Jeniese Hosey
@Jenesaisquoithe

I love fashion and I've never let my size dictate what I wear or don't wear. I like to think of my style as chic and put together. Truth of the matter I'm willing to try anything fashionwise at least once.

Photographer: Issac Nun at SUB URBAN CREATIVE

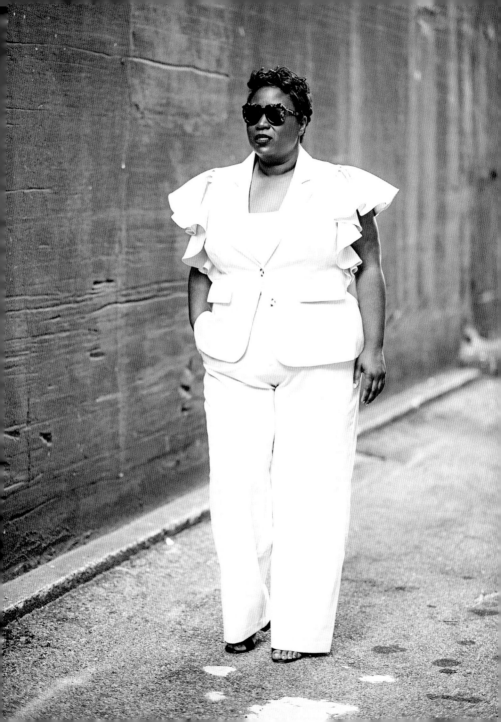

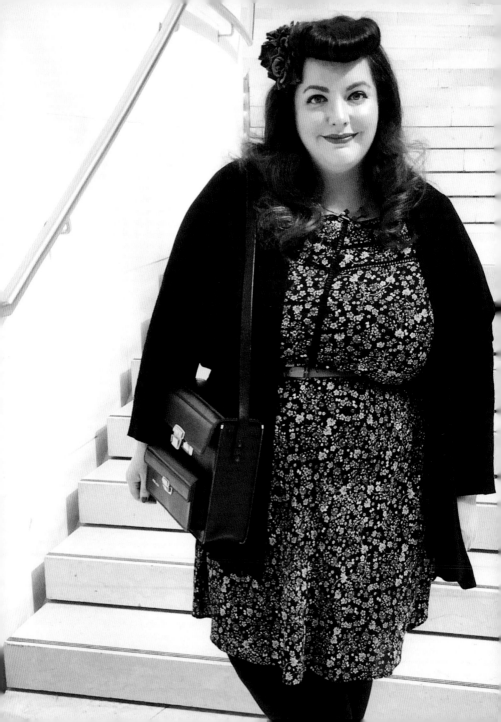

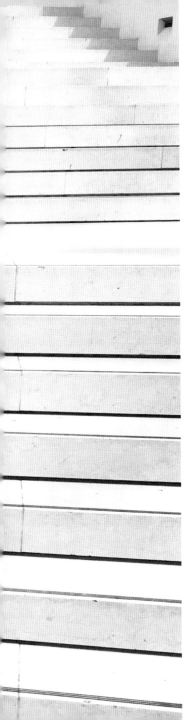

+
Diana Thompson
FashionLovesPhotos.com

*I really enjoy mixing vintage
finds with current trends to
create a modern update on some
of my favorite style notes from
yesteryear. I'm a sucker for old
camera bags as handbags and
have yet to meet a pocket dress or
floral print I haven't liked.*

+

Abby Hoy
@thepennydarling

I have been in theater my whole entire life — so my wardrobe (and my personality!) were all about finding the spotlight! I love the retro and whimsy that old school Broadway made famous. I describe my style as a mix of Broadway glam mixed with Lucille Ball with a dash of glitter for good measure! It's definitely made me more confident on and off the stage!

Photographer:
Preston Schreffler

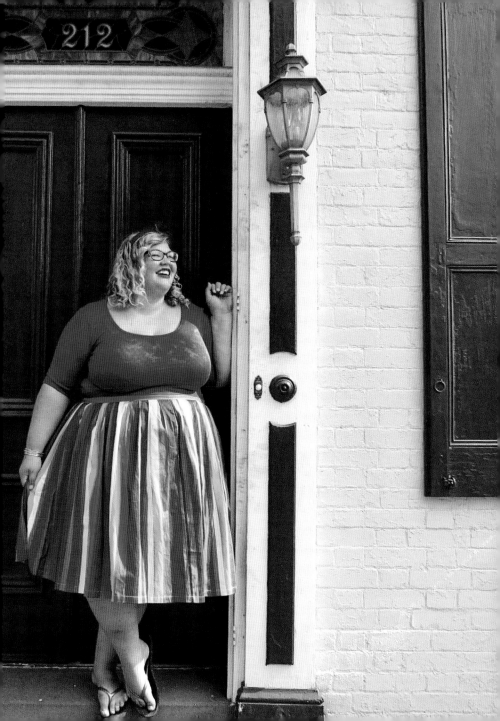

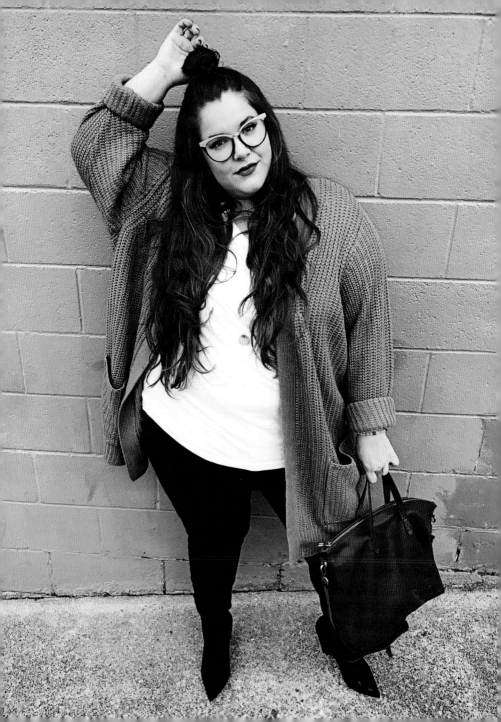

Natalie Hage
@NatalieMeansNice

My style is a little bit of wannabe soft goth mixed with a sprinkle of hipster and a whole lot of FUCK YOU to anyone and everything that told me I couldn't wear what I wanted to. Every outfit I wear is a defiance to the society that would rather push me down than build me up. I can build my own self up now.

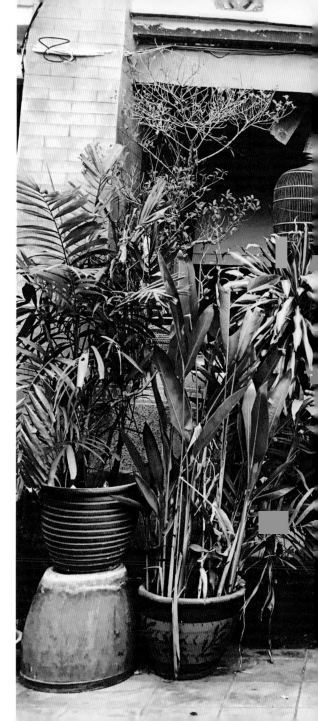

+
Nazirah Ashari
@NazirahAshari

*Black is still THE color, modesty
is still the essence, but that
edginess and that cream color
hijab I got going is the sign that I
represent a new generation
of Muslim women, unstereotyped,
updated. We dress however
the heck we want.*

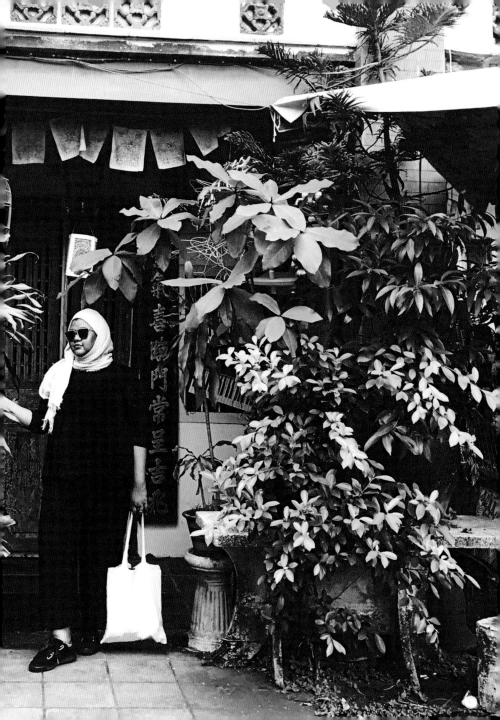

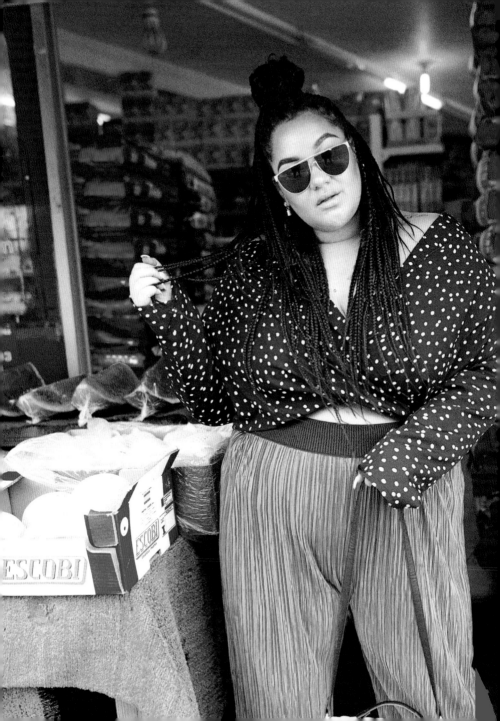

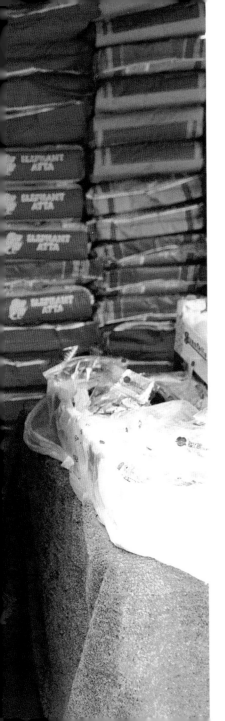

✛
Gracie Francesca
@GraceFVictory

I've only really found my style recently which some might find surprising. I like color, big earrings and statement shoes. I also like to be comfortable so that's always a factor when I'm getting dressed in the mornings.

Photographer:
Jade Keshia Gordon

Corissa Enneking
@FatGirlFlow

My style is some kind of '90s Mariah Carey meets sensible carpool lane mom. I care about comfort first and foremost and want my clothes to allow me to be myself. I can't be myself if I'm tugging on my clothes and wondering if everything is in just the right place. I like styles that just let me be me.

Photographer: Kelsey Kimberlin

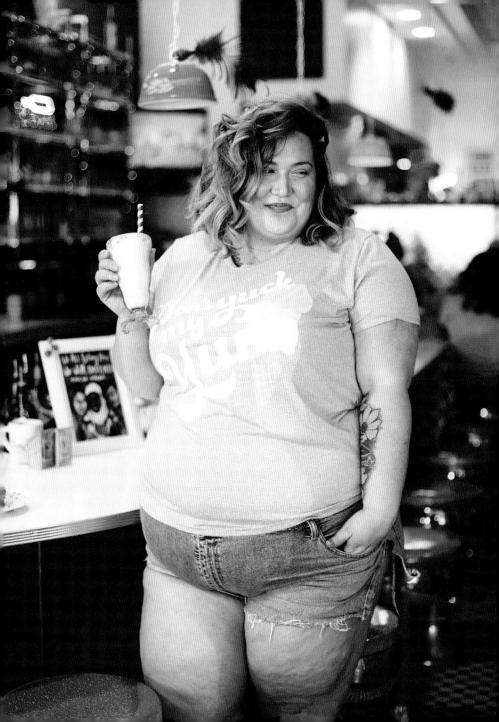

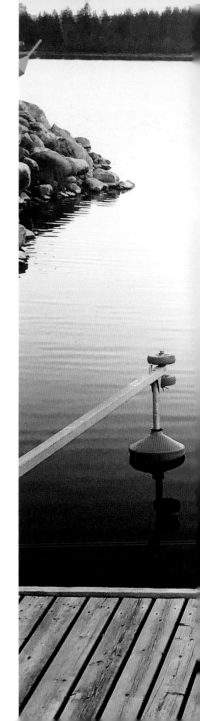

+
Christina Lovgren
@valflickan

Fuck flattering!
No rules, just style!

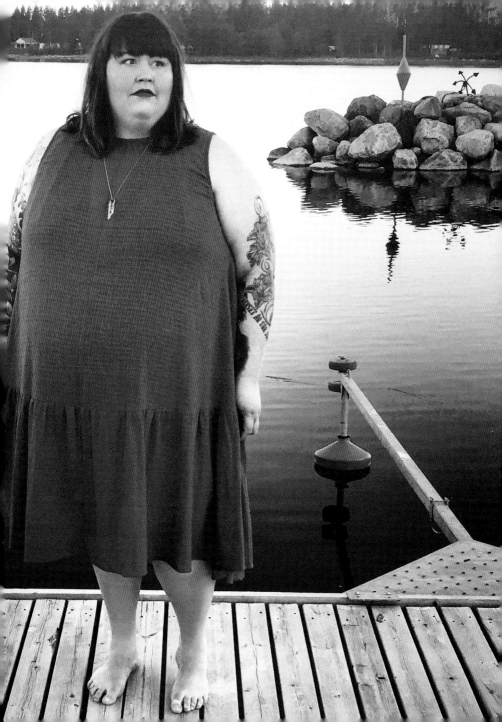

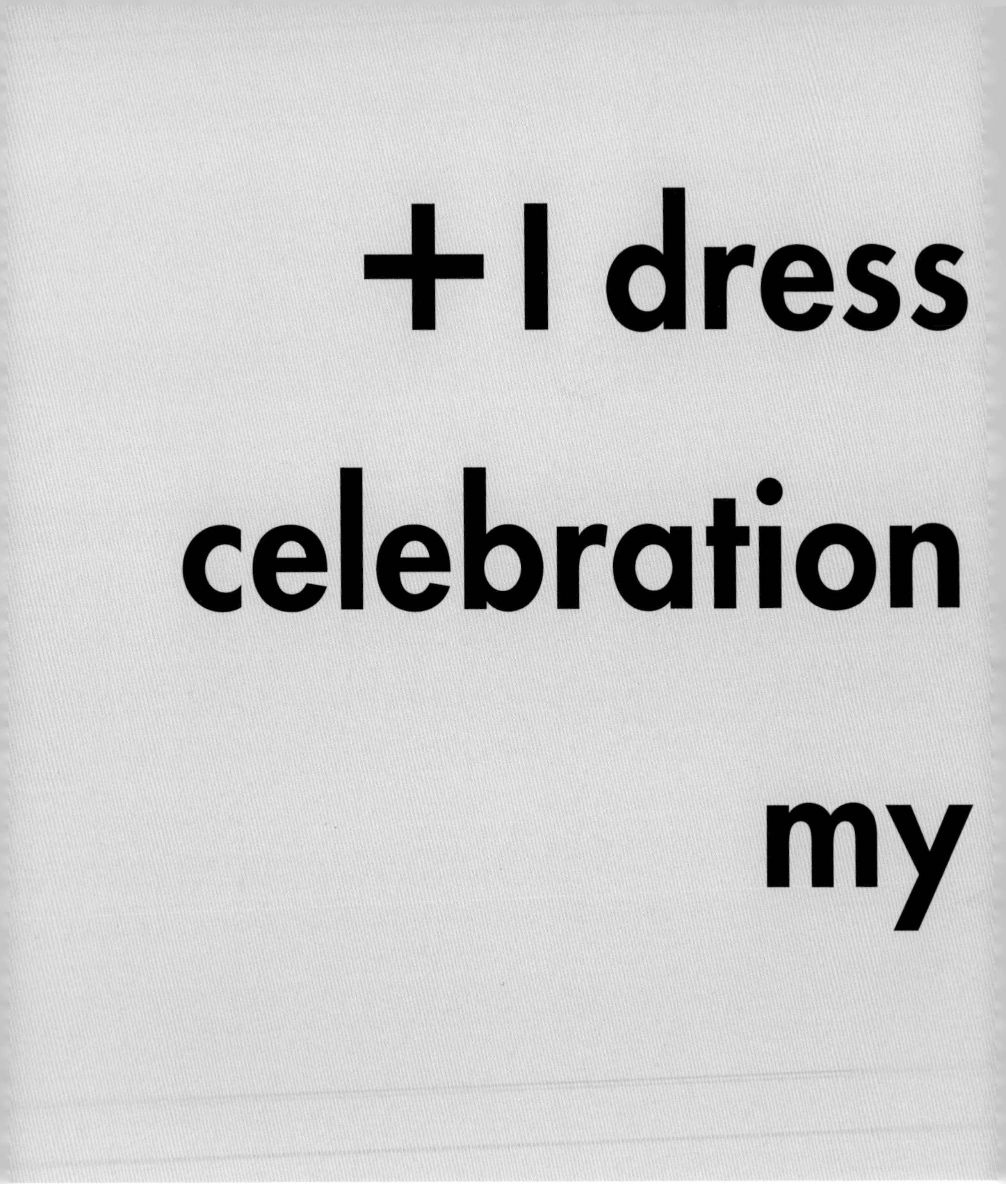

+I dress

celebration

my

for the

I want

life to be.+

—Cynara Geissler

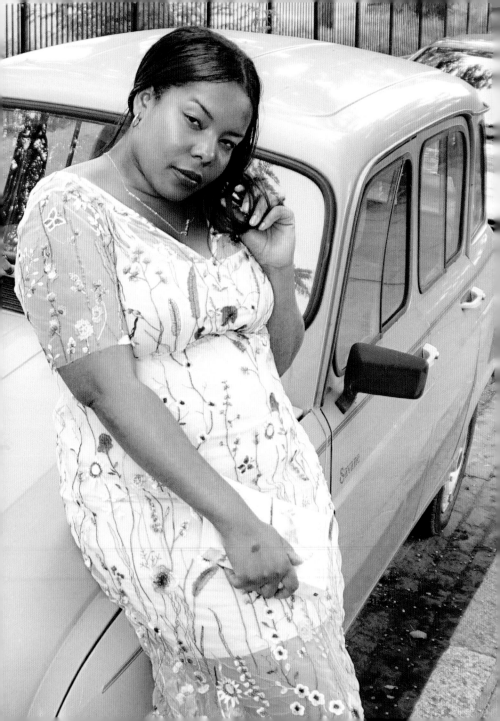

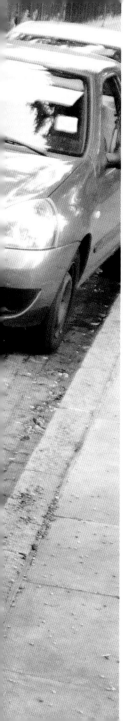

Chloe Pierre
@chloepierre_ldn

My style is practical, stylish, feminine (at times) but most of all true to me. I am a firm believer in urban being a trend which never goes out of style, and it very much represents my own style in every way — it's real!

Photographer:
Christine Roberts

Stacey Louidor
@HantiseDeLoubli

Many people tell me fairly regularly that they wish they were able to be like me and wear what they want with "such confidence" and even though they mean well, to me that is the worst backhanded compliment. My style is carefree because I want to live my life as a carefree fat black girl. We exist and I'm always happy to serve as reminder.

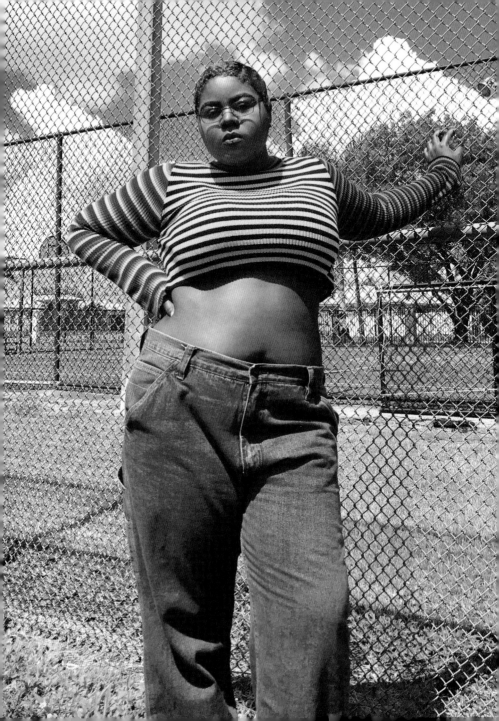

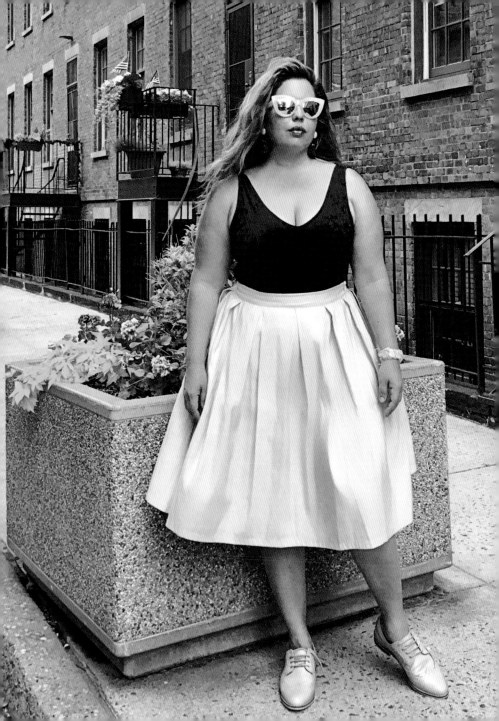

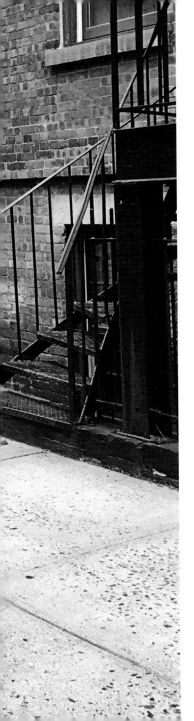

+
Fluvia Lacerda
@FluviaLacerda

*I'm probably one of the worst
people to talk about trends.
I wear what I want,
when I want, however I want.
Dressing for myself is the
only rule I understand.*

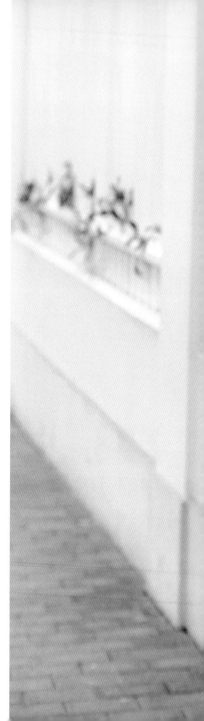

✛
Aileen Melendez Salinas
@OurEmpathie

I love to wear what I like, without fear to say, I like to be versatile in terms of colors and styles, I love pink but there are also days when I love black. I dress according to my mood and I love it.

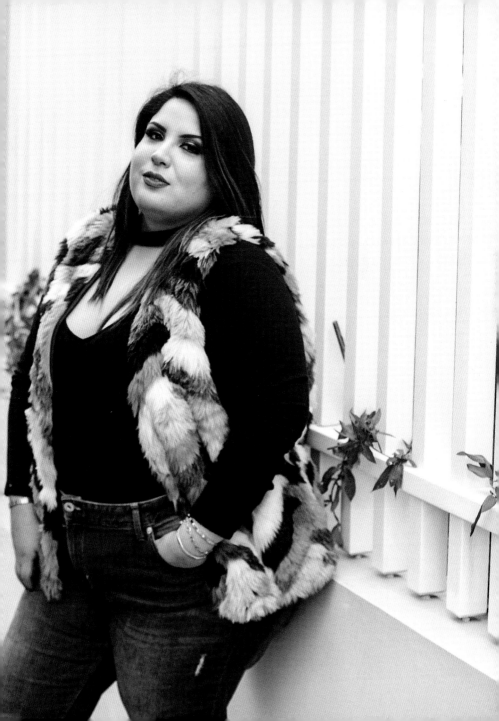

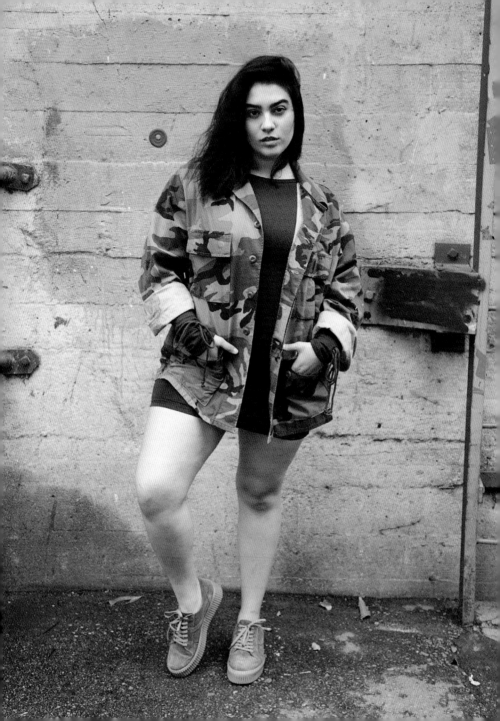

Nadia Aboulhosn
@NadiaAboulhosn

I love combining form-fitting pieces with something oversized. Keeping one piece plain/neutral but the other with a dope print.

Danie Vanier
@daniellevanier

*I favor a more minimal look
which is still quite hard to
achieve in plus sizes so it means I
need to be creative with my style.
But I can't resist mixing in some
great prints and luxe fabrics with
that sharp, streamlined style.*

Photographer:
Jade Keshia Gordon

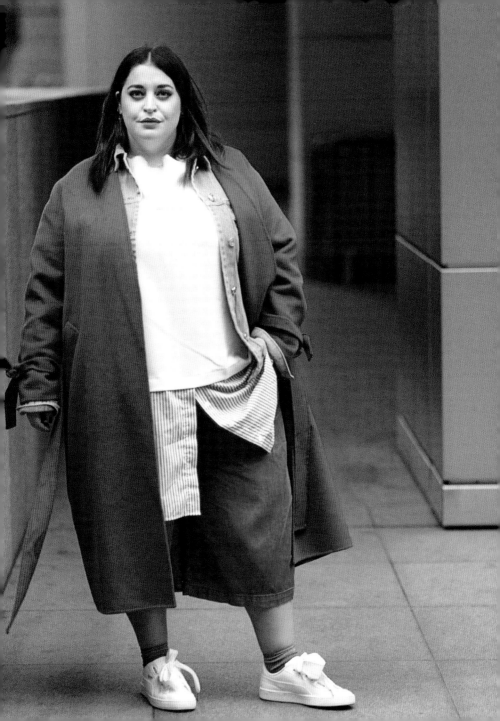

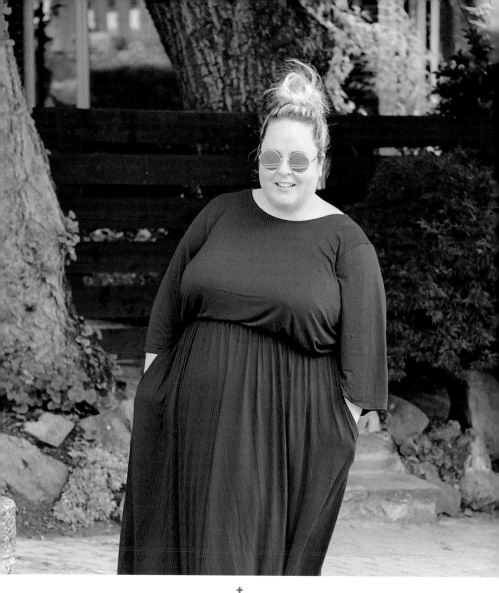

+

Hanna Suhonen @HannaWears

Scandi-inspired style with oversized items and block colors,
mostly neutrals with pops of color.

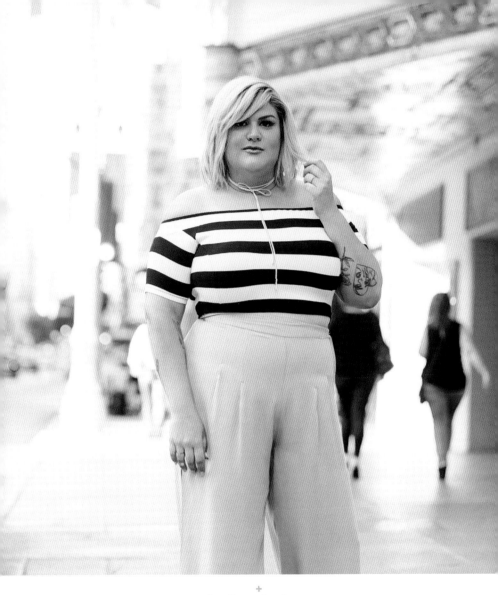

Nicolette Mason @nicolettemason

I think my style has been informed by my queer femme identity and growing up in Los Angeles and New York City. It's a little bit of glamour with a lot of edge. Fashion has and will always be a platform for my self-expression, and I've loved all the many ways it has evolved over the years.

Photographer: Elton Anderson

Ella Tkach-Dreazen
@kimoorella

My favorite outfit is self-confidence because it never wears out.
I love trying new looks and making every style work for me.

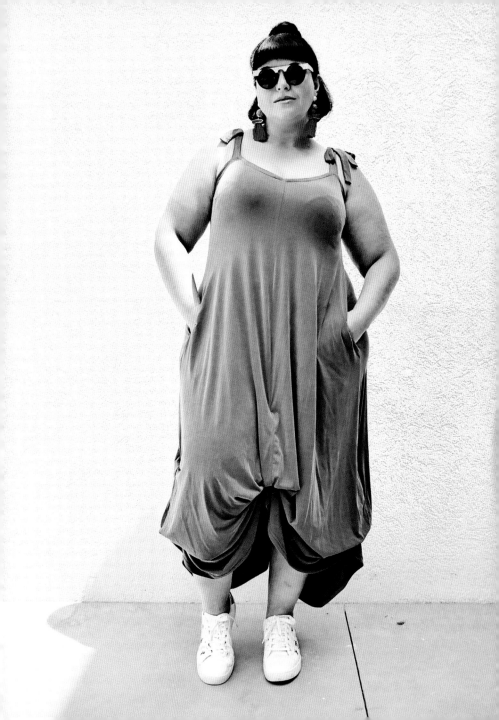

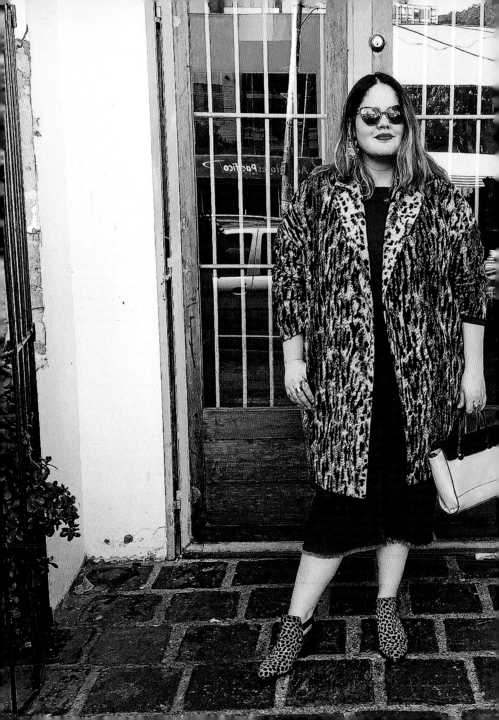

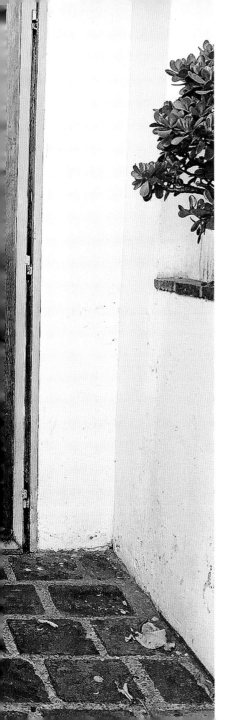

Adriana Convers
@fatpandora

*I would define my personal style
as in a state of constant pursuit.
Over the years I have realized
that we should not believe in
the rules and when the people
say "don't wear that." My style
is based on challenging myself
with color, prints and silhouettes.
My style is, look for my essence
among the sea of options offered
by fashion.*

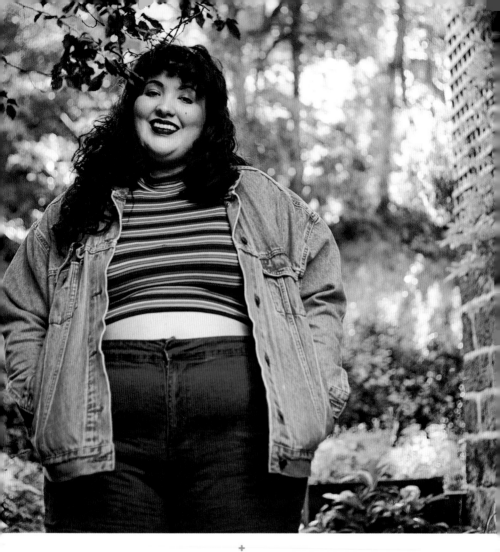

Marie Southard Ospina @mariesouthardospina

I wear things that are loud and that get me noticed. Because, really,
there's no shame in taking up space with my fat body, or in being seen.

Photographer: Paddy McClave

+

Gaëlle Prudencio @GaellePrudencio

My style is about breaking the rules and embracing my curves with a touch of African print.

Photographer: Danielle Ahanda

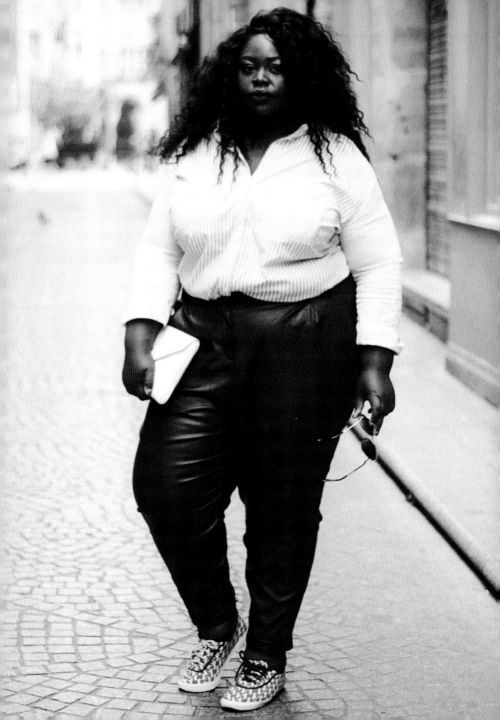

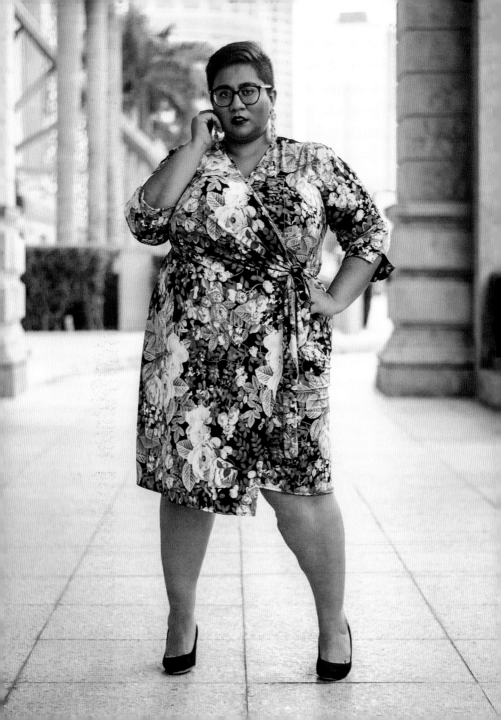

Ratna Devi
@SapphireSplendour

I am a tomboy at heart and that's how I would define my style, it always includes a casual tee and jeans but on days where I feel like I could dress up a little more a bright patterned dress and stripes are what I love as well! I don't think I have a concrete sense of style; it's very fluid and based on how I am feeling and what I am inspired by at the moment!

Photographer: Megan Wee

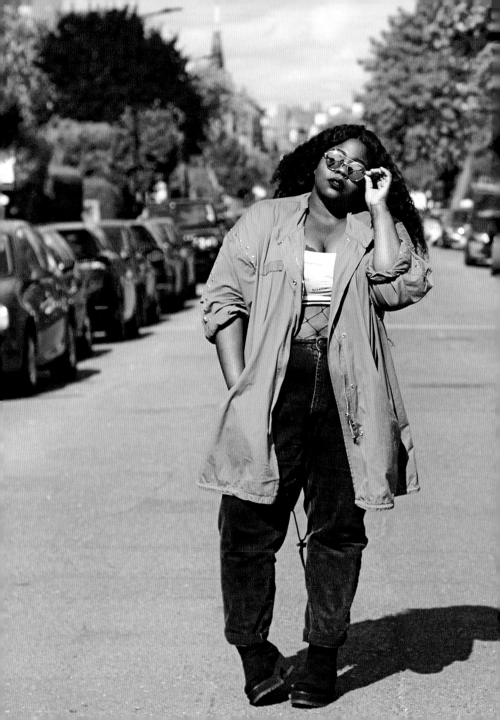

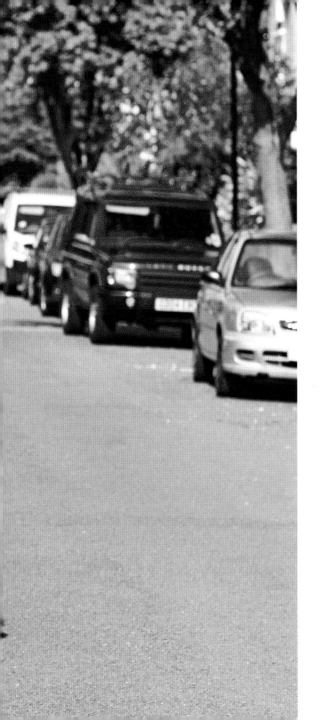

Stephanie Yeboah
@NerdAboutTown

*I'd say my style is quite fluid,
and totally depends on my mood
that day. A lot of the time I
tend to lend myself towards edgy,
'90s-inspired pieces that
are comfortable and versatile.*

Photographer:
Eran Fagura

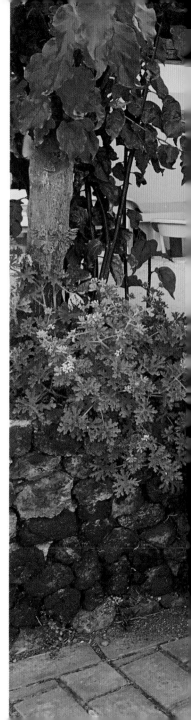

Alysse Dalessandro
@readytostare

My personal style is very much about standing out. It's gaudy. It's over-the-top and it's unexpected for someone my size. My personal style is about refusing to hide or change who I am to fit anyone else's comfort zones. I dress for me!

Photographer:
Kristen Strickhouser

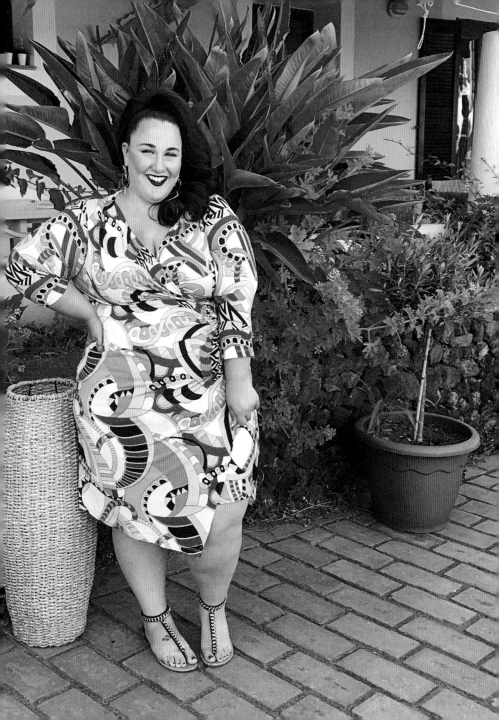

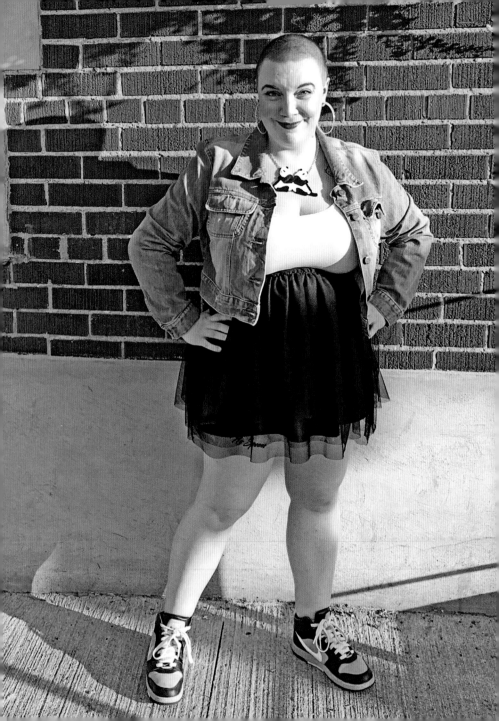

Aggie Sems
@plussizepanda

I have two sides: I'm either super cute or super sexy. My style is best described as "pastel goth on a rap video set."

Photographer: Cadyn Forbes

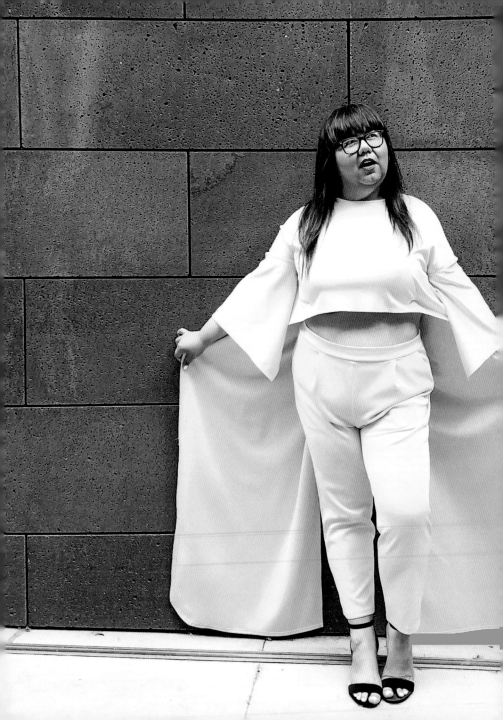

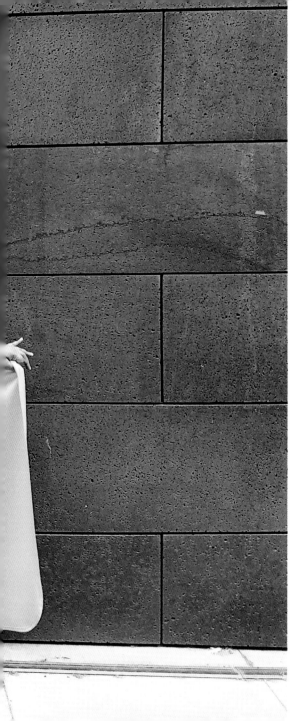

Virgie Tovar
@VirgieTovar

*My style is big attitude and tiny
dresses. I'm all high contrast,
bold prints, bright lipstick, huge
earrings, and an astounding
variety of sunglasses (which
I wear over my prescription
wayfarers to stay true to my nerd
roots). I use fashion to have fun
and provoke response and think of
my exposed belly, arms, cellulite
and cleavage as indispensable
accessories. My icons are Miss
Piggy, Dolly Parton, Stevie Nicks
and Honey Boo Boo. I'm inspired
by scenes like Alphabet City circa
1993. I always ask myself: "Is it
loud, cheap and likely to make
a lady clutch her pearls?" If yes,
then I'm wearing it.*

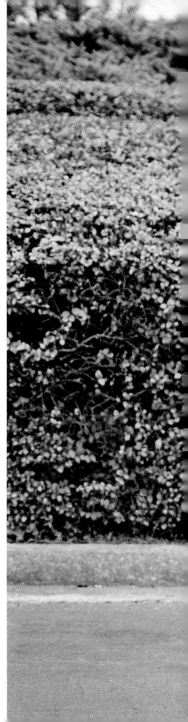

Marie Denee
@MarieDenee

My style? I am definitely a free spirit with my style, going with my varying Virgo moods. BUT, what I do find myself drawn to are clean lines, monochromatic styling, fitted pencil skirts, and everything with an ease of comfort and style. I do not take it too seriously and like to feel amazing in whatever I wear!

Photographer:
Chase Reign

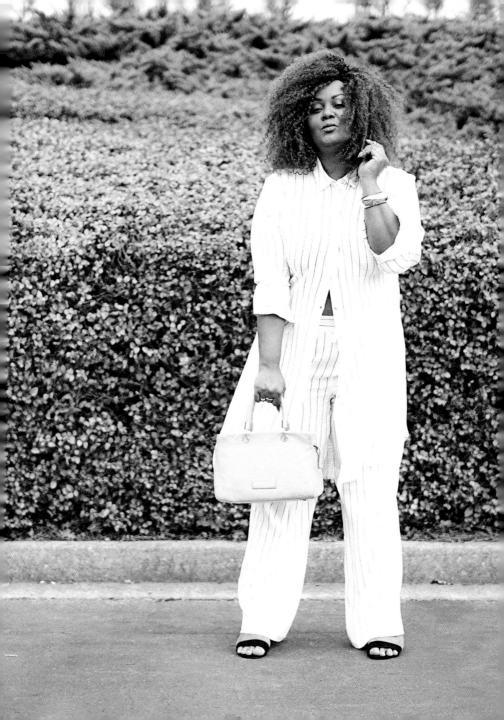

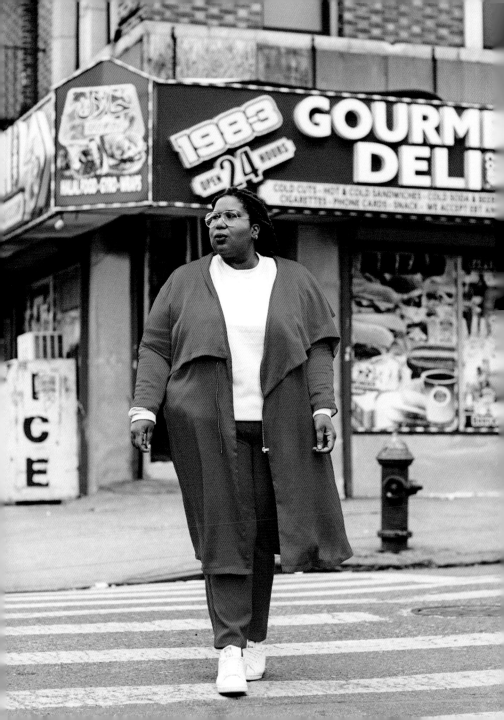

Kellie Brown
@AndIGetDressed

*Style is not measured in
the size of your jeans.
All women can be inspired.*

Photographer: Lydia Hudgens

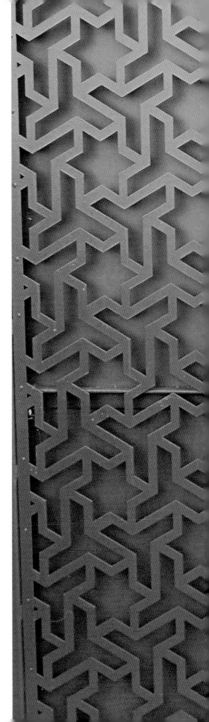

+

Tracy Broxterman
@Brxtrmn

My style has evolved within the last few years into what I dub "weirdo mom": mixture of black on black textures, all with the ease of flow-y jersey and peppered with exaggerated hardware and accessories.

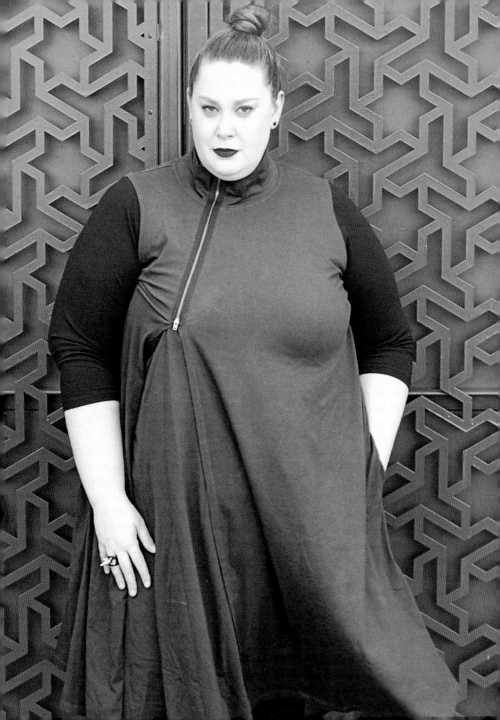

+ I have just
have turquoise hair,
in tattoos and
"fashion forward" as
who weighs half

as much right to

be covered

be considered

any woman

as much as I do.+

—Christina McDermott

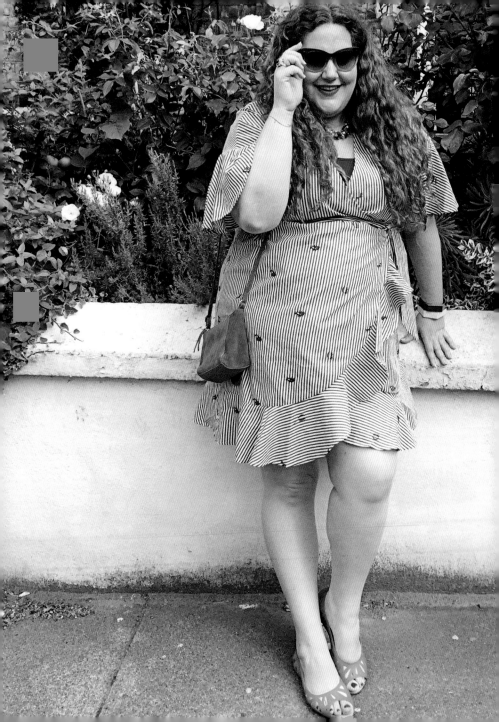

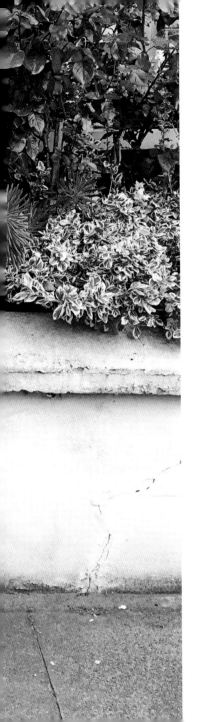

Hayley Stewart
@CurvesnCurlsUK

*I think dressing should be fun —
my style is colorful and girly.
I'm a big fan of prints, and I
like to inject a bit of whimsy
into my outfits. I also insist on
being comfortable. I can't
stand high maintenance outfits
that are a pain to wear.*

Ushshi Rahman
@Ushshi

At various points in my life my outfits have had much to say about what identities I occupied: be it man-eater or psychobilly queen or, as Kendrick says, an "antisocial extrovert." The more streamlined, rooted and mature my life becomes, the more I veer into minimalism. I still bust out full-on "looks" if my mood dictates it but I no longer feel pressured to perform, a luxury I feel most fat girls aren't afforded.

Photographer: Travis Rivera

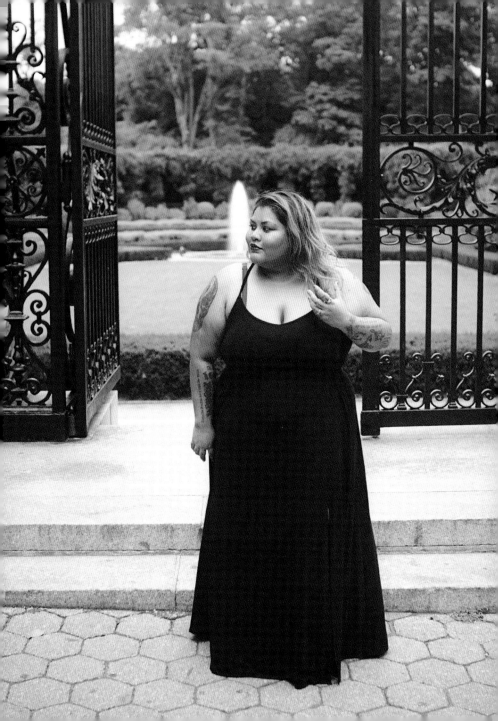

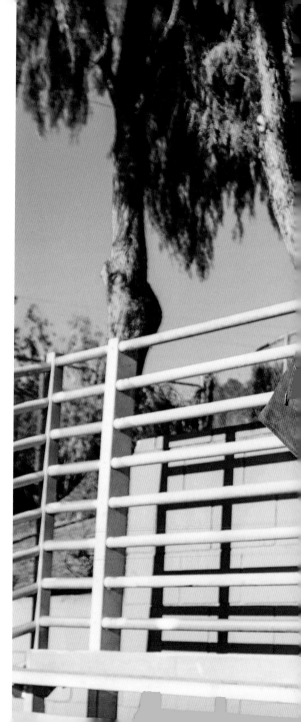

April Quioh
@AprilKQuioh

*My personal sense of style is a
reflection of my Liberian heritage,
my commitment to always being
comfortable, and my hectic
lifestyle. I don't wear things that
poke my skin, uncomfortable
shoes or limiting patterns. I wear
clothes that feel like me, allow
me to move through the world
with ease, and often look like
something Solange would wear to
the grocery store. And I love
to show off my shoulders!*

Photographer:
Vanessa Acosta,
@fromabolivian

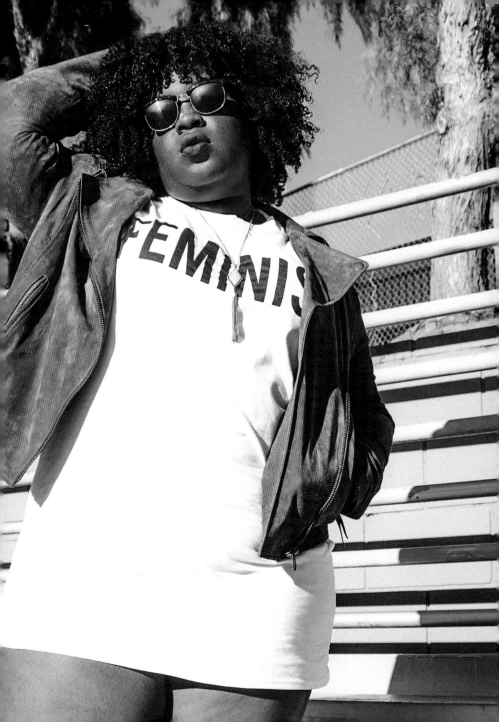

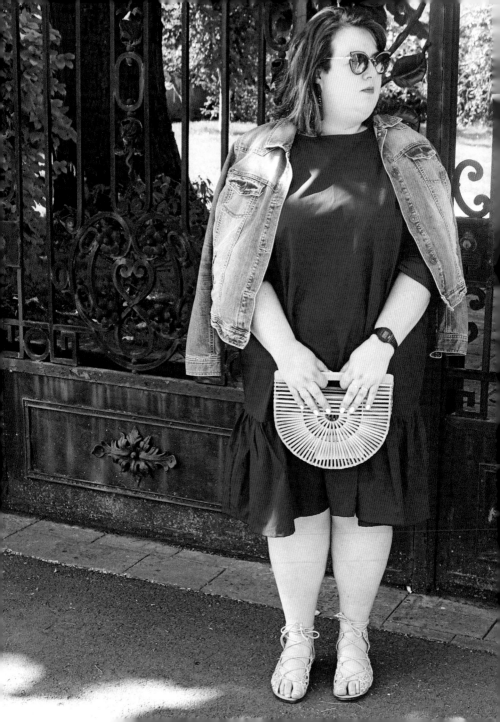

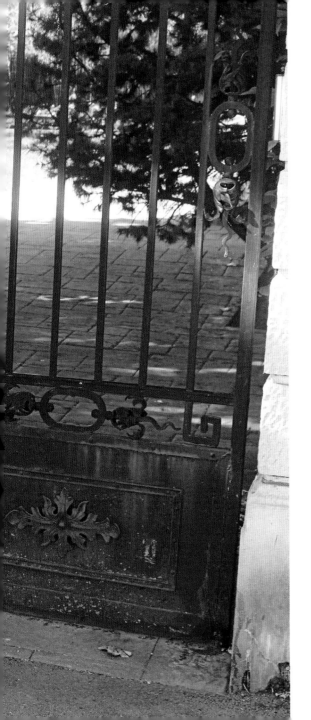

Jessica Carballo
@ABitOfJess

*I like to keep it classy,
but I like it more when I
inject a little fun.*

Amanda Elliott
@amandaapparel

My style is perpetually changing, and I love to serve a variety of different looks. Today my ensemble includes soft textures in pink and pastel tones, but tomorrow I might be wearing pleather and leopard print! What's most important to me is that my garments fit well and that they match the vibe I want to radiate on a particular day.

Photographer: Lianne Mackay

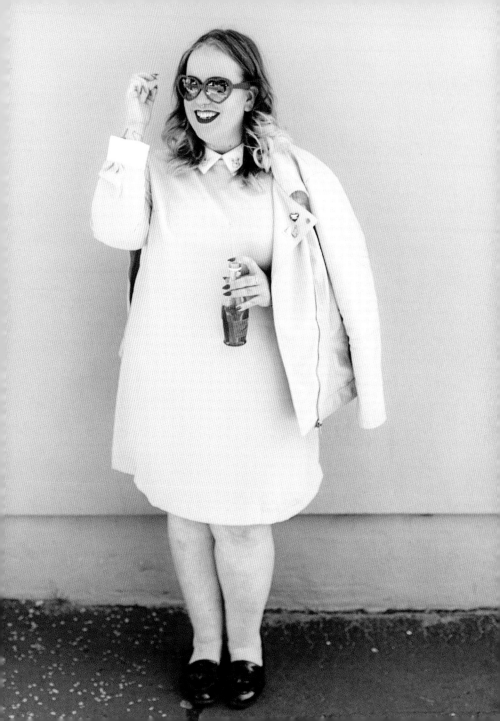

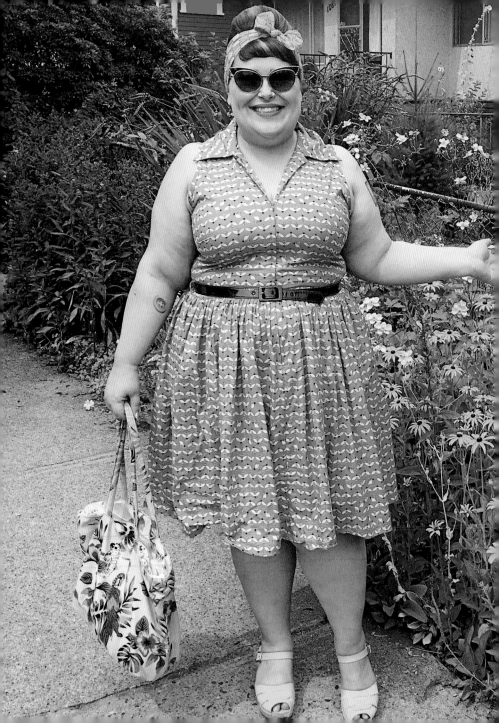

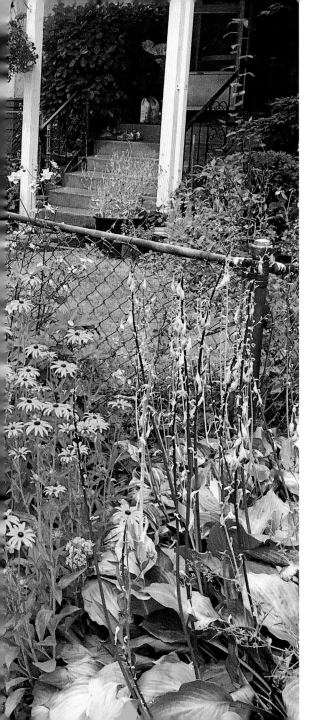

Cynara Geissler
@Cynaragee

I dress in what I call Toddler Grandma Style. In our culture we don't expect toddlers and grandmas to dress for the male gaze so they have a lot of sartorial freedom — no one expects toddlers or grandmas to wear a uniform of neutral skirt suits and high heels. I love bright colors, novelty prints, mixing patterns and textures, full skirts, and lots of oversized accessories — excessories — and prefer oxfords and sneakers. Toddler Grandma Style is about questioning and expanding what it means to dress like an "adult." I don't think dressing like a grown-up has to be quiet, boring and contained.

Photographer:
Don English

+
Isha Reid
@Pic_Pixie

My style blueprint tends to lean towards dresses, particularly in the vintage/vintage-inspired spectrum. It may sound quite restrictive, but I love experimenting with different prints, colors, textures and structures. For me, the most important thing is feeling good in what I'm wearing. If I'm feeling good I feel like I can conquer the world.

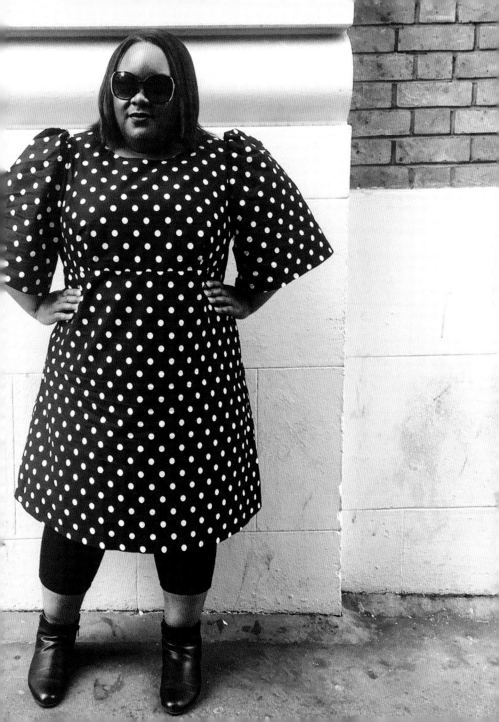

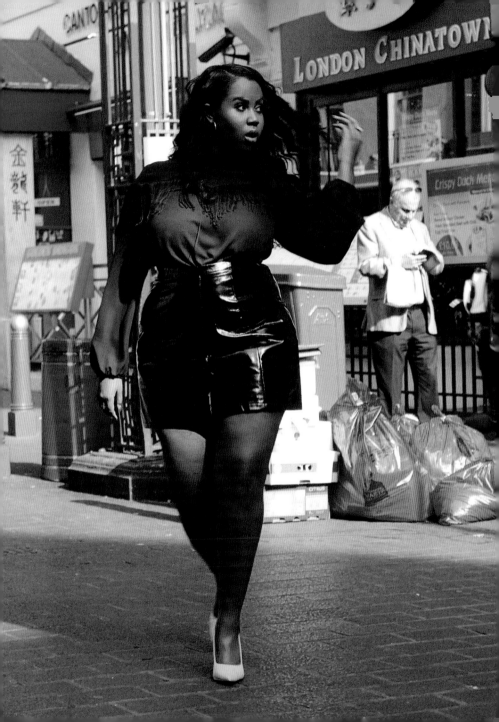

Lauren Nicole
Coppin-Campbell
@LaurenNicoleFK

I'm always evolving and reinventing my style! I'm a lover of fun, fashion-forward trends combined with key basics. I've learned to build and set my outfits with accessories: bags, shoes, jewelry . . . . If they're bold and bright, they're me!

Photographer: Aminat Adenuga

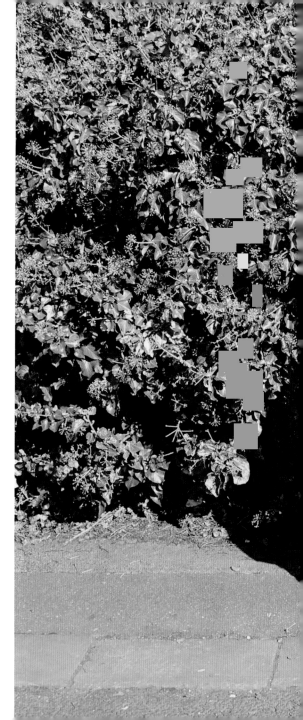

✚

Em Smyth
@TerribleTumbles

I have two style settings: The first is "Your grandma's wardrobe" — I live for knitted rollnecks, nerdy skirts and woolen tights (if autumn was a person I would be it). The second: Joan Holloway — think tailored pencil dresses, big hair and a red lip. Either way, whether it be via a '60s print or a '50s silhouette, I never feel properly dressed unless I'm giving a nod to the past.

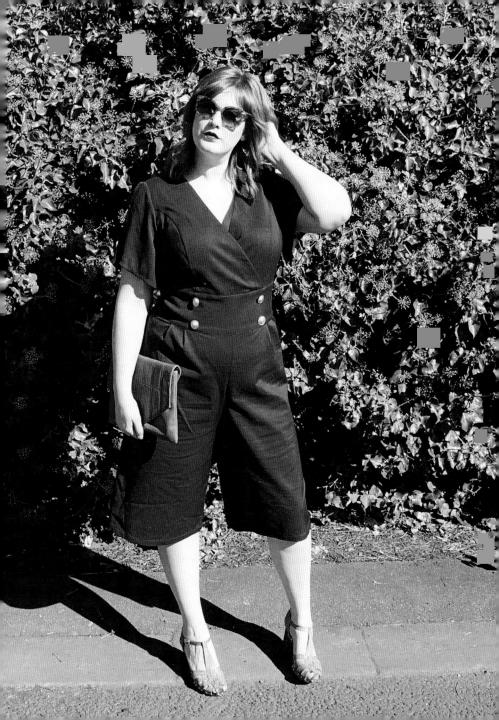

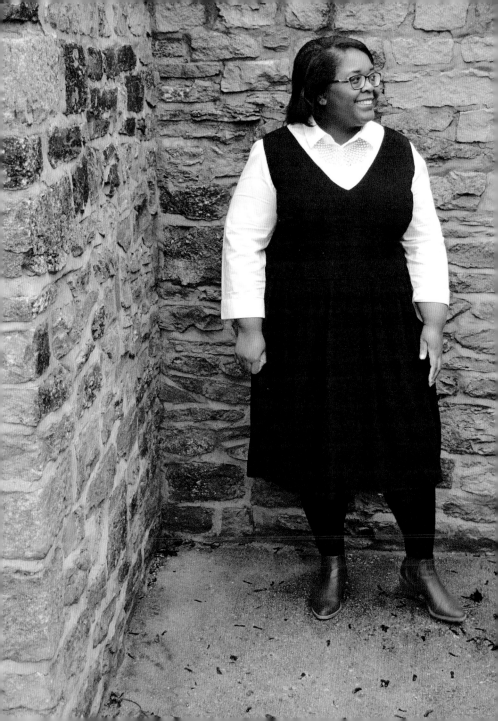

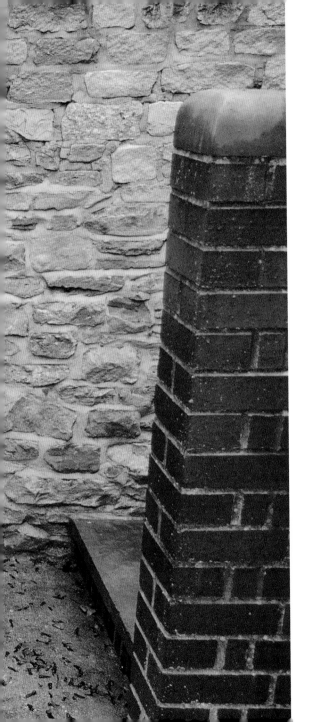

✛

Natalie Ellis

@awheelbarrowfullofstyle

*I wouldn't say my style is smart,
smart casual, on trend;
it's a mixture of everything really.
It's just me!*

Zoë Meers
@IKIWN

I definitely favor classic shapes, which I think comes from years of second hand / charity shopping and having to pull together great outfits from what is available there in plus. After wearing black so much when I was younger, my favorite outfits are now the most colorful ones which I'll ALWAYS finish off with big statement earrings and bright lipstick. As much as I love to clash my prints and patterns, I'm actually never happier than when I've achieved high levels of matchy-matchy!

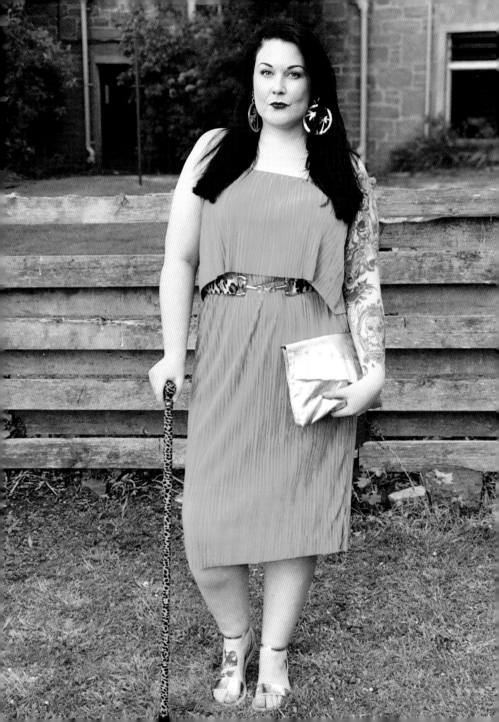

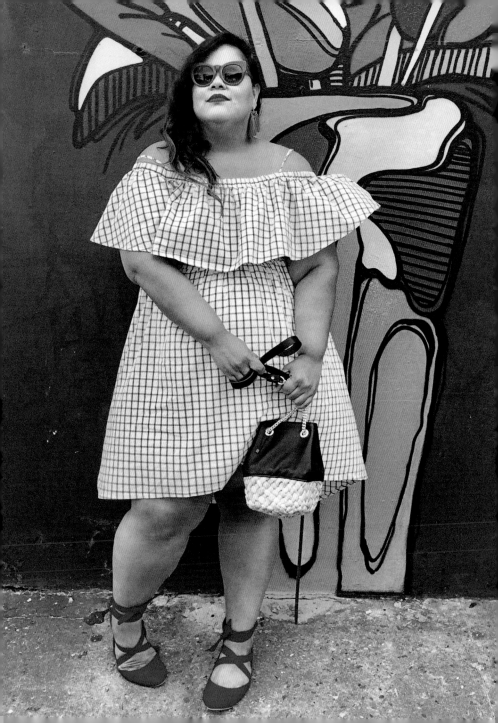

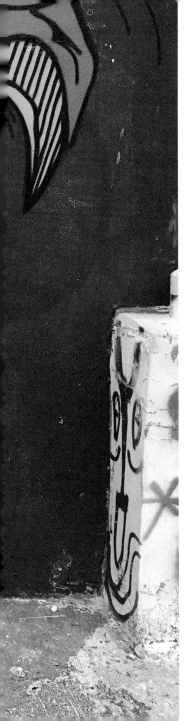

Nadynem Ortiz
@Nadynem

*A summer dress in my
tropical island is a must
all year round.*

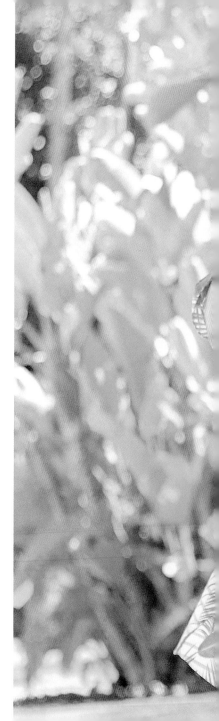

Reah Norman
@StyledByReah

My style is all about being comfortably chic. My wardrobe is full of pieces that I can work in, play in, mix and match, and style in versatile ways that work for my industrious lifestyle. Polished and current, without compromising comfort.

Photographer:
Rachel Richardson of
@lovelyinla

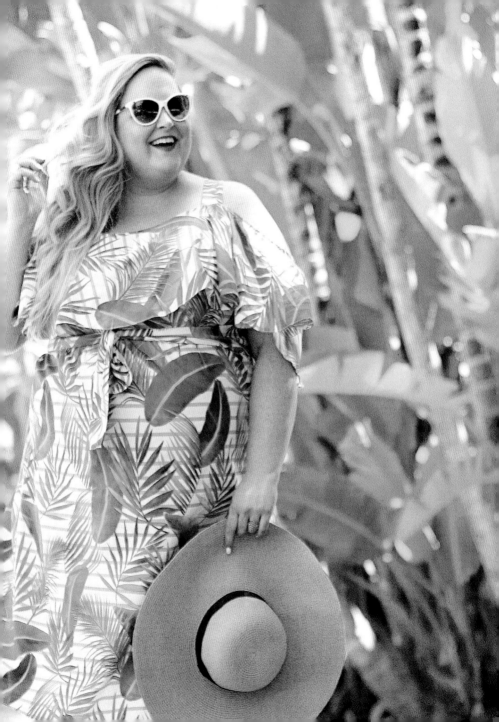

Thulisa Mkhencele
@ThickFitAndFabulous

I consider my style as being simple, fun and comfortable — most of the time I spice things up to make my outfits interesting to feed the eye of those deciding to look. Most of my looks are vintage inspired, I'd like to think with a fun, boho, androgyny and sporty vibe going on.

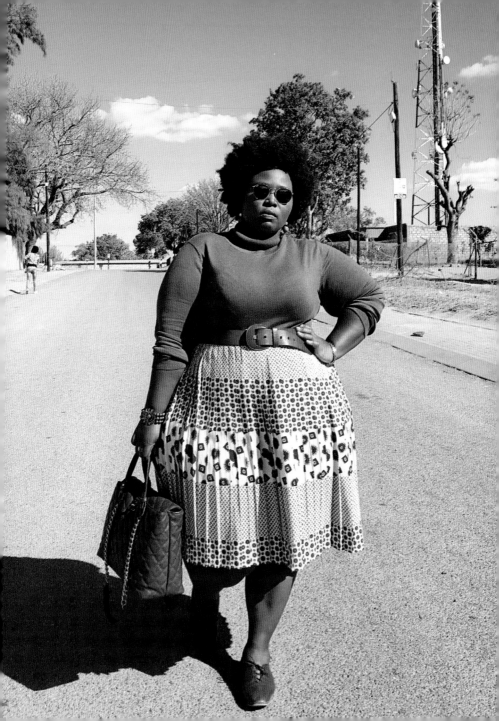

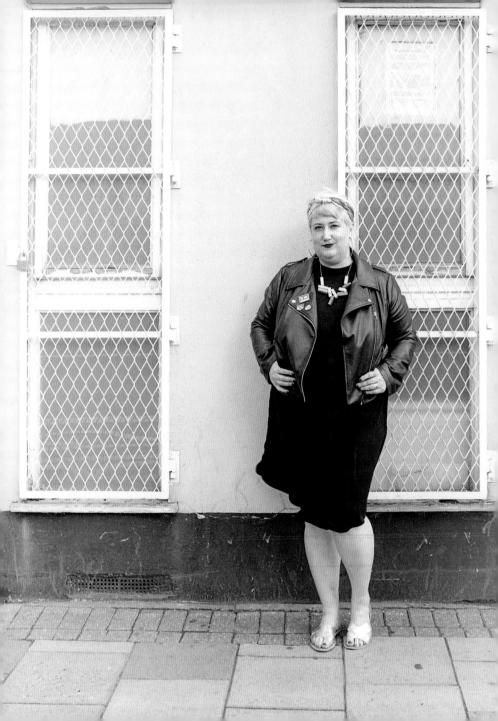

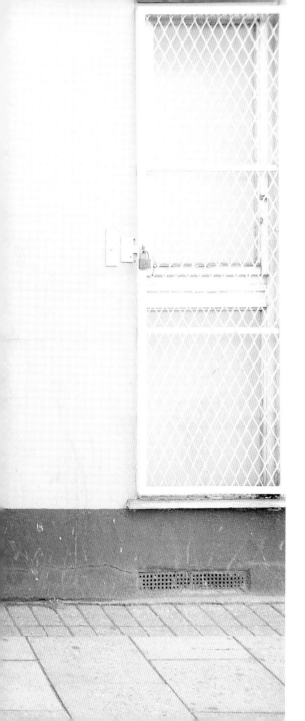

✛
Christina McDermott
@ChristinaMcMc

*I've always been fascinated by how
fashion ties into identity. When
I open my wardrobe, I ask myself
who I want to be that day. As I've
evolved as a person, my sense of
fashion — and identity — has evolved
too. I've been everything from a
1950s pin-up girl to the kind of
'80s goth who sat around burning
patchouli and listening to early
Cure records. At the moment,
I'm veering more towards bright,
bold and colorful, like some kind
of obnoxious fashion magpie.
As fat women, we're often told that
we should hide in hanky hems
and butterfly prints if we want to
be heard and taken seriously.*

Photographer:
Dan Barker

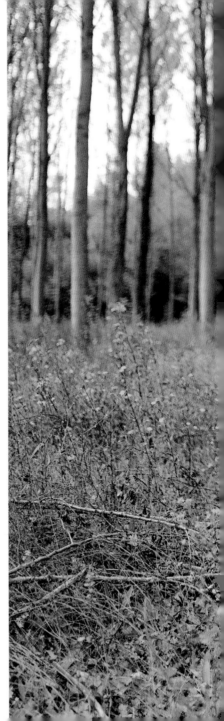

+

Virginie Grossat
@FreakyUseless

*My style is always changing —
it goes between sweet, rocky,
sexy, preppy, because a plus-size
girl can be anything now.*

Photographer:
Jean-Philippe Gimenez

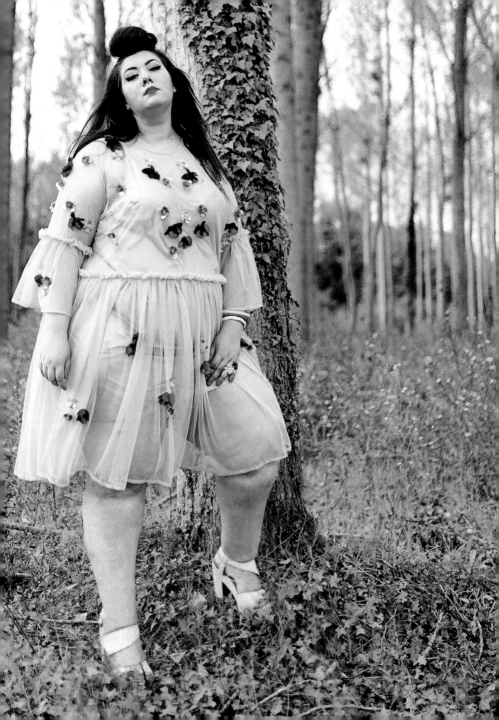

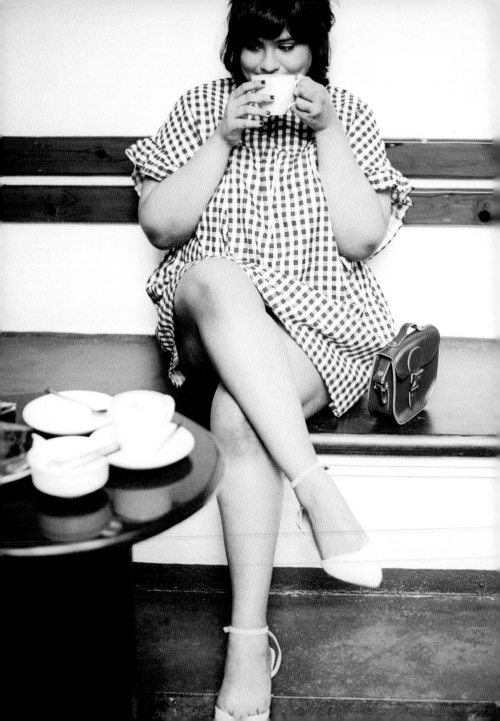

Ragini Nag Rao
@KittehInFurs

For me, style is about adding interest to my everyday life. From a head-to-toe costumey outfit to artfully cut basics that stand out, style is what elevates the mundane to something deliberate, considered, thoughtful. And it's not just confined to my wardrobe. Style is the particular language of aesthetics that permeates everything I choose to incorporate in my daily life. My rule of thumb is, if I love it then it's definitely my style.

Photographer: Taha Zaidi

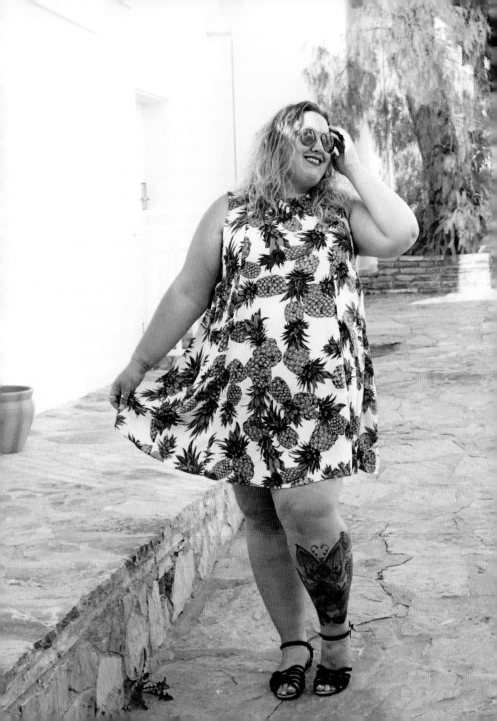

Kitty Morris
@KittyRamblesALot

*How would I define my style?
A friend once described me as a
sort of Heavy Metal Hello Kitty,
which is probably pretty accurate!
I love girly dresses and tutus,
hyper feminine styles, combined
with that punk rock edge, faux
leather jackets, vegan combat
boots, chunky silver jewelry. I'm
heavily influenced by music, even
my wedding dress was inspired
by Guns N' Roses' "November
Rain." I like to feel powerful in
what I wear, while also wearing
things that are adorable.*

Photographer:
Stu Morris

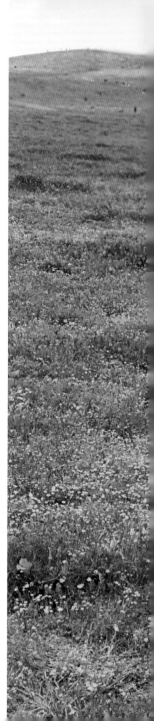

Sophia Carter-Kahn
@ShesAllFatPod

*My style is kitsch witch — friendly,
fun, colorful, with lots of black
and crystal jewelry mixed in.
I don't worry too much about
being trendy or about NOT
being trendy — I just enjoy getting
dressed and the tactile joy of
fashion. I used to wear only
things fat people were "supposed"
to wear — cinched waist, dresses
that are more like tents. Now I
wear whatever I want. And I love
to wear a red lip!*

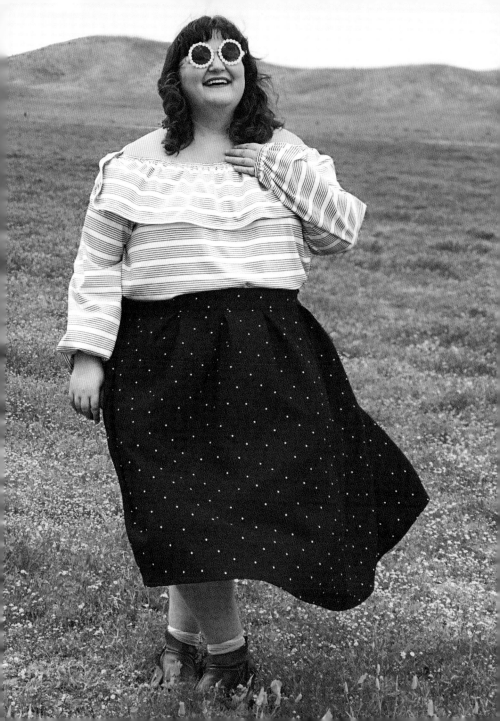

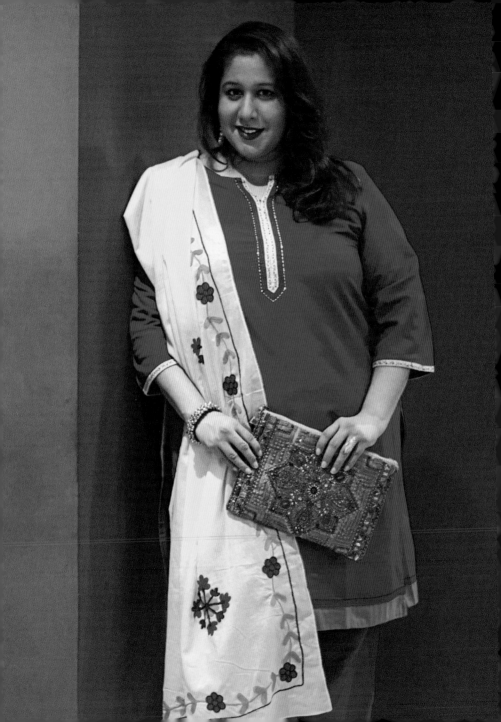

Amena Azeez
@fashionopolis.in

Glam and statement-making — that is how I like to describe my style. I love to color block with vibrant colors, mix bold prints, pair Indian and Western silhouettes together, layer my statement necklaces and stack up my arm party. When it comes to fashion I am a quintessential maximalist at heart who strongly believes in go big or go home.

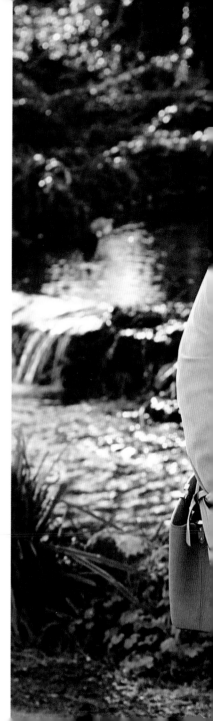

+
Chloe Elliott
@chloeincurve

My style is romantic and feminine with a little modern tailoring — but above all it is centered around comfort. I like to look put together without feeling restricted or uncomfortable.

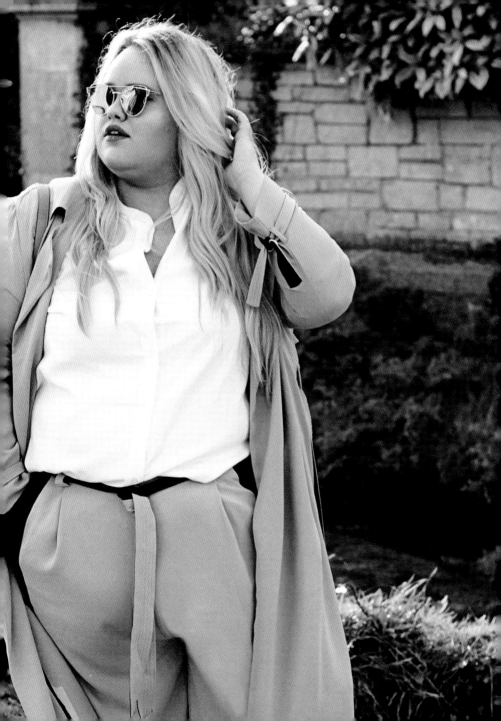

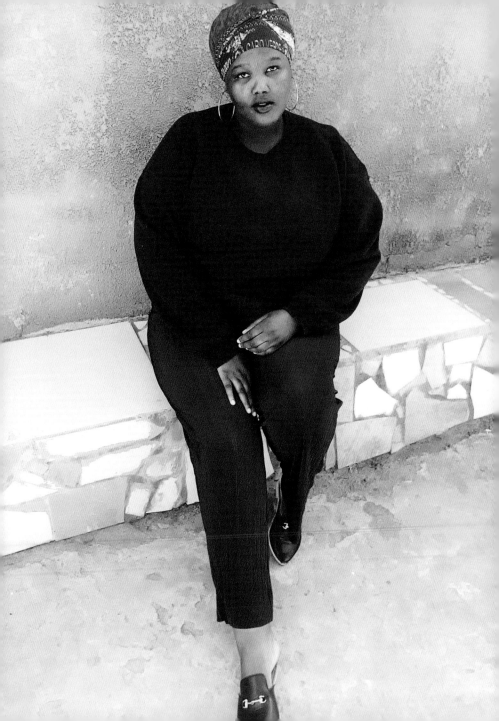

Nomali Minenhle Cele
@NomaliFromSoweto

I battle with putting my style into words because I have always battled to get the clothes I want or that will make me feel like I'm dressing like myself. My style is quite functional — affordable, multi-wear, comfortable — with a cute something thrown in. The skirt might be comfy but I'm gonna wear that crop top just because. Oh, and I love hoop earrings and a surprising lipstick, which are the "something cute" on the days when I can't be bothered with interesting clothes.

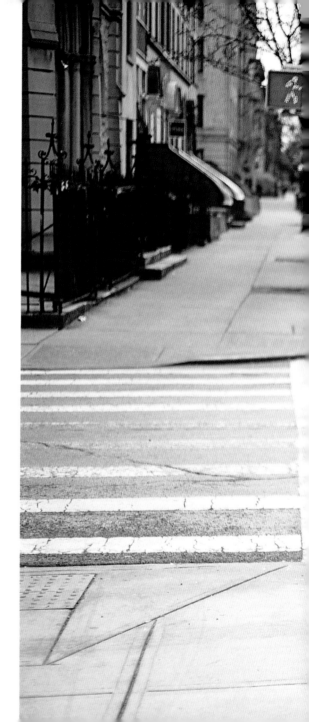

+
Rikke Klint Jørgensen
@StickySweetDanish

*My style is a bit eclectic as it's
made up of so many different
trends and influences. I dress
according to my mood and
whatever tickles my fancy.
I like to stand out, but I also love
to be casual and comfortable.
I'm always influenced by the
Scandinavian minimalistic way
of dressing, sprinkled with a bit
of rock chick and a lot of Rikke.
Think lots of black, denim,
sneakers or brogues, cute socks
and a ton of lipstick. Oh, and my
ever-changing hair color!*

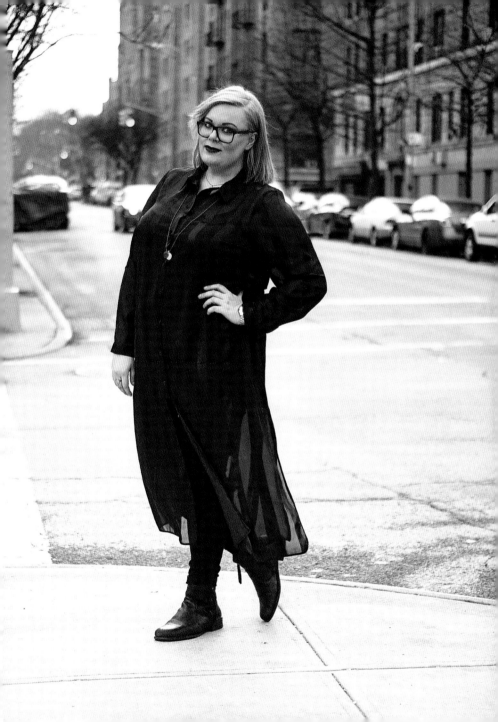

+ Wearing things that every lump show I'm so in love and the ways in me move

accentuate
and bump is how I
with my body
which it helps
through this world.+

—Nadia Mohd Rasidi

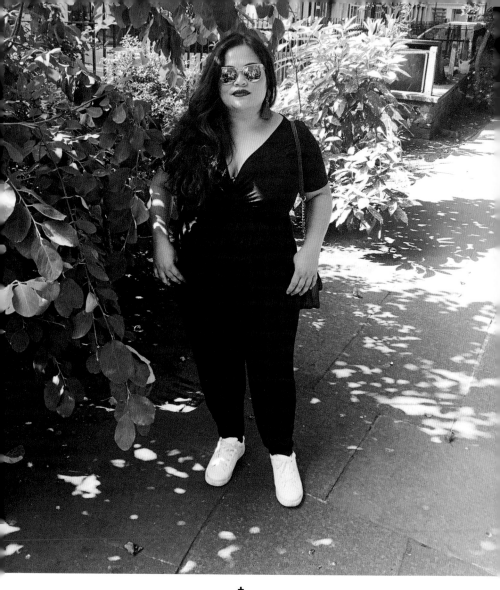

+
Nadia Mohd Rasidi @nrasidi

Growing up fat in Malaysia, my style was limited to "whatever hid me best." If stores didn't think it was worth carrying my size, I didn't think I deserved to look or feel good in what I wore. Today, I still dress for comfort, but my version of "comfortable" has changed.

Photographer: Lana Huh

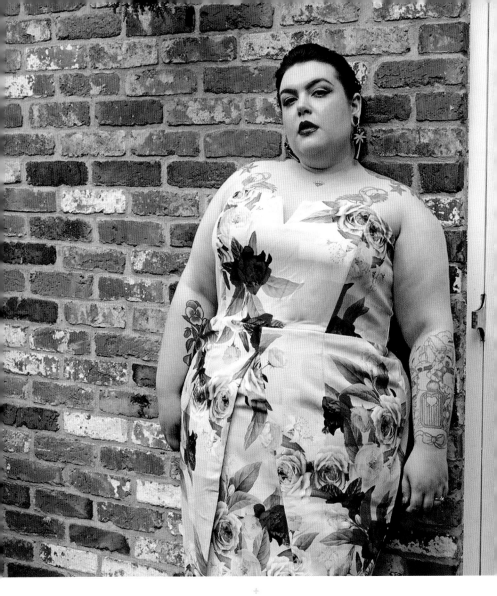

Nancy Whittington-Coates @SugarDarlingBlog

I love juxtaposition in my outfits, I think because I feel like me being a fat person who loves fashion is in itself an oxymoron in society's eyes. My style signature I would say is bold makeup and loud trainers teamed with dressy clothing.

Alexandra Smyrliadis
@Final_Destination666

I like chains, drama, weird textures and dark lips — I think of my style a bit like if someone made a Barbie that was half Marilyn Manson, half Mariah Carey.

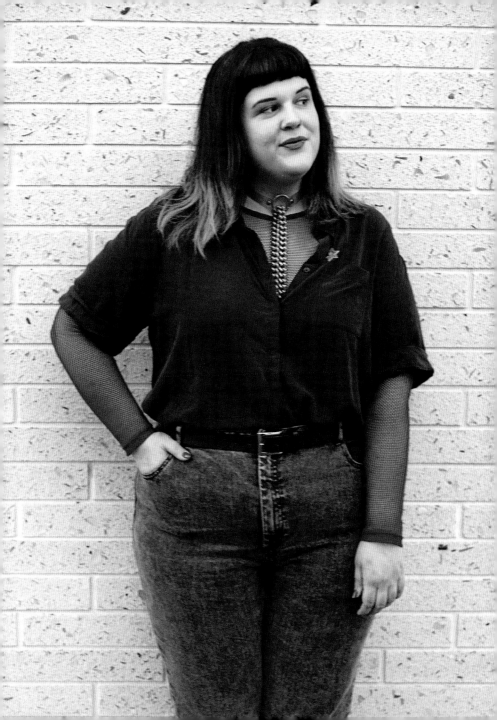

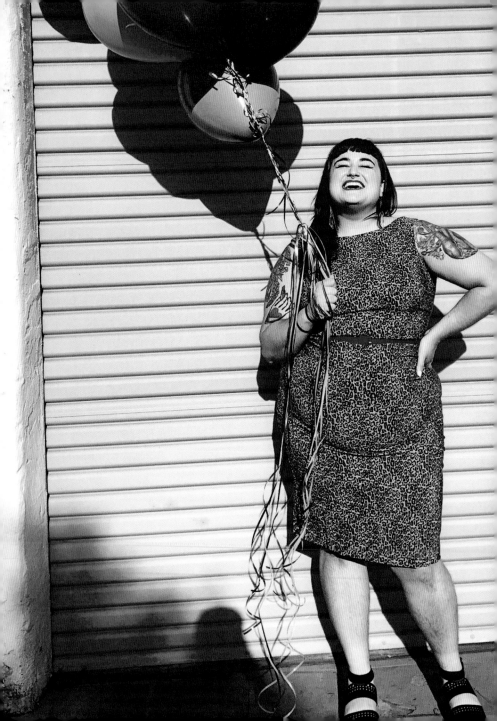

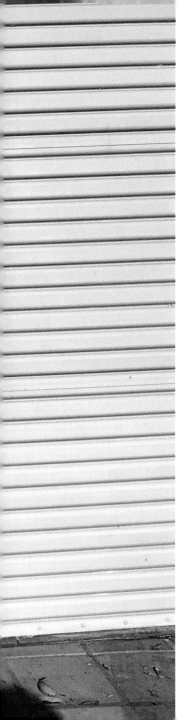

+

Nikki Padula

@The.Ample

I inhabit fashion by playing around in it! I treat clothing and femininity as costume — it's all about experimentation with decades, personas, colors. Take what speaks to you and leave behind what doesn't.

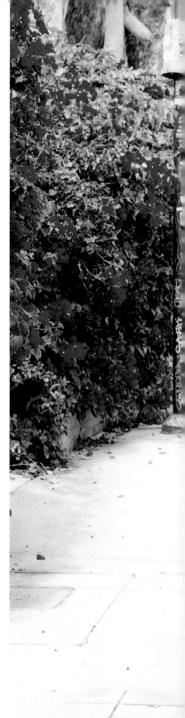

+

Simone Mariposa
@SimoneMariposa

*Fashion helps me show
gratitude to the power
and beauty of my body,
and the colorful and
carefree nature of my
personality at the same time.
#WeWearWhatWeWant*

Photographer:
Jade Keshia Gordon

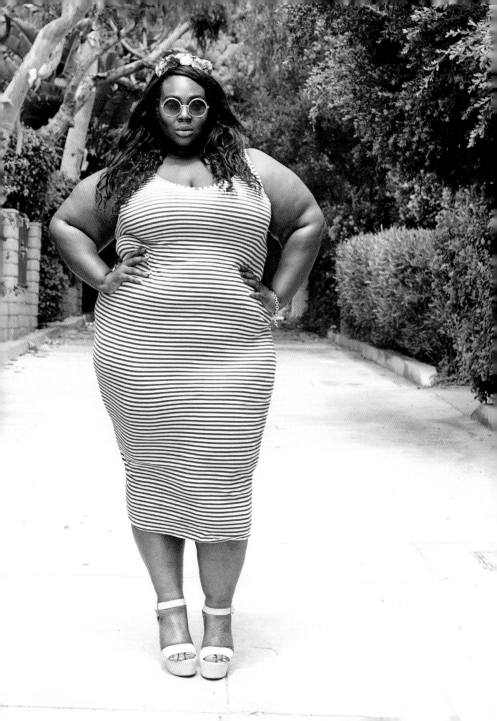

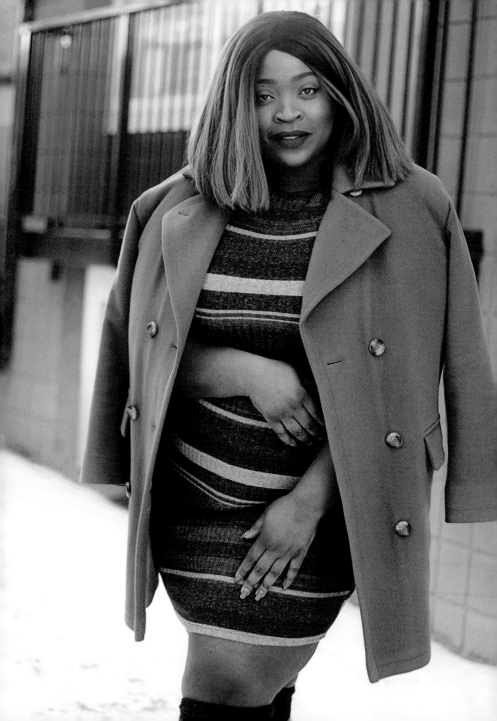

Inemesit Etokudo
@InemesitEtokudo

My personal style can be summed up in three words: print-mixing minimalist. Greatly influenced by the diverse cultures I have experienced traveling the world, my eye for bold colors and ability to mix diverse patterns earns me my signature look. I am never one to shy away from dressing outside of my comfort zone, refusing to conform to outdated plus-size fashion "rules," in hopes of inspiring other plus-size and curvy women to do the same.

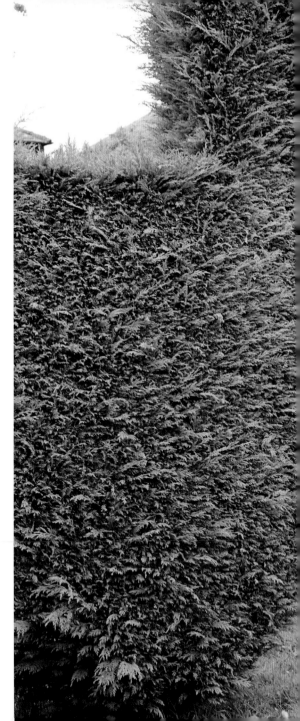

Stephanie Lawson
@StephanieDJL

I think of my personal style as balanced; not diverse enough to be eclectic, yet not defined enough to confine to one aesthetic. When plus-size clothing options began to expand, I found myself dressing as ostentatiously as possible just because I could, with little regard for how the outfits made me feel. Now, I gravitate towards neutral colors and minimal accessories as this is where I feel most stylish.

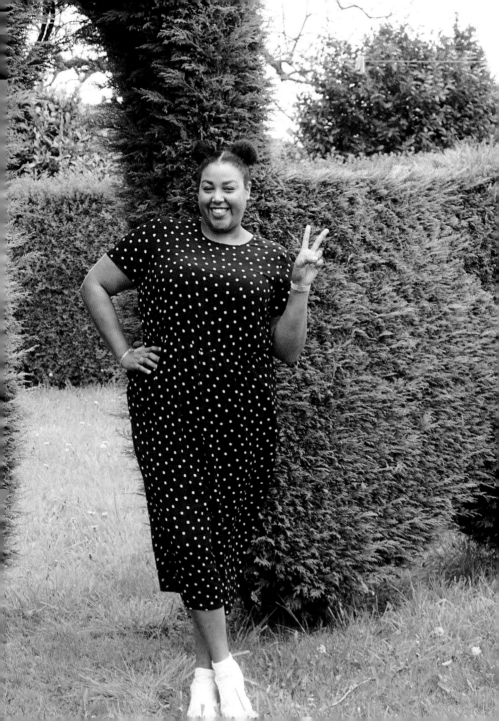

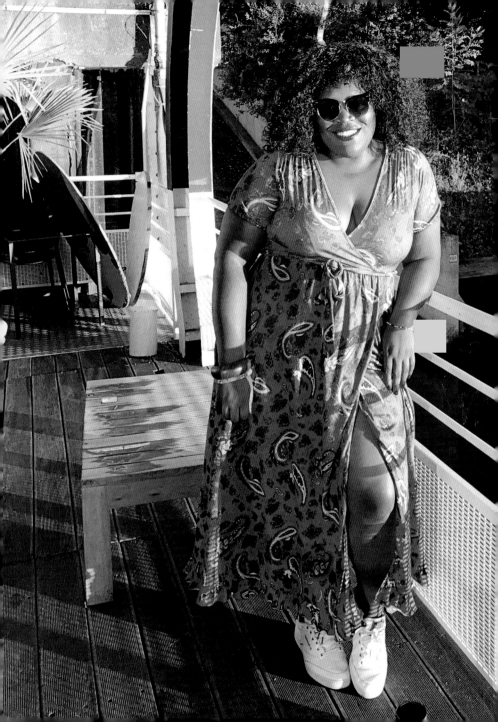

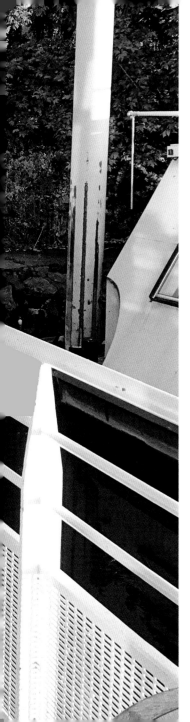

Dominique Kenmogne
@pomelokiwie

*I would say I've no specific style.
It depends on the days, on my
mood, on what I want to express
on that day . . . . The only thing
really important to me is enjoying
and playing with clothes,
with fashion.*

Meagan Kerr
@ThisIsMeaganKerr

I don't subscribe to so-called fashion rules — sometimes I wear figure-hugging bodycon, sometimes I'm all about the loose and flowy. My style is constantly evolving and a reflection of how I'm feeling; I think that fashion should be fun, and while black, stripes and gray feature often in my wardrobe, different textures make my wardrobe far from boring.

Photographer: Doug Peters at Ambient Light

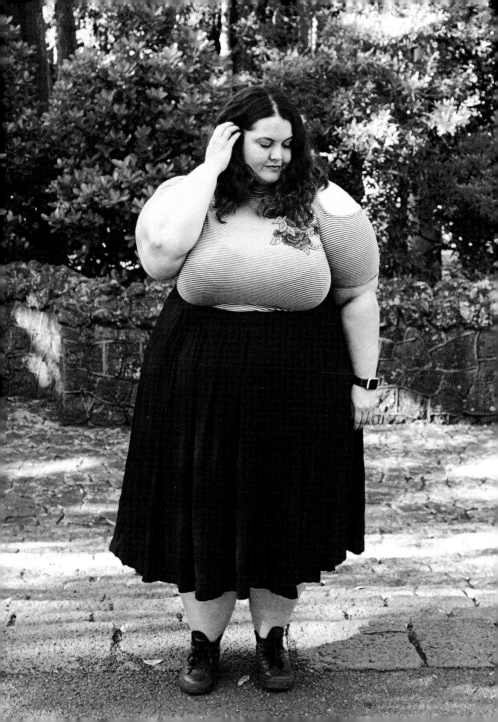

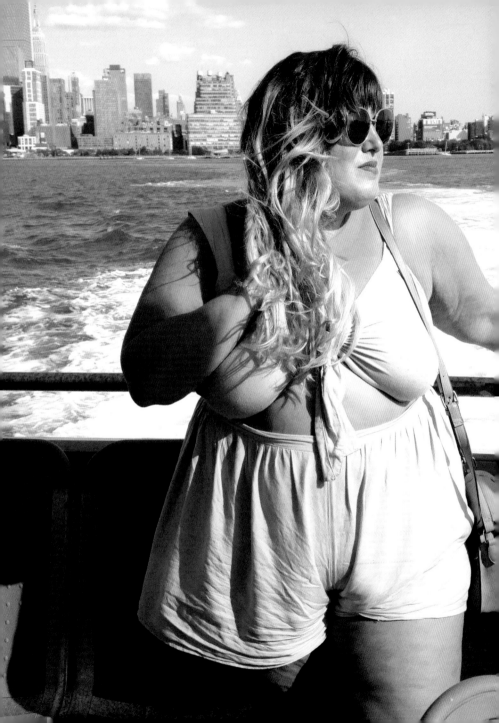

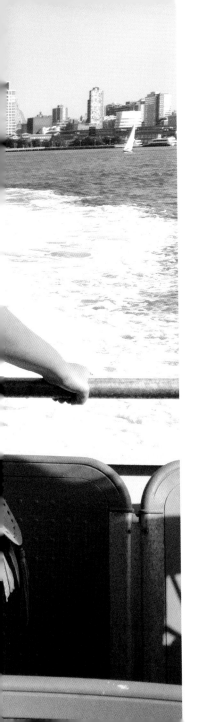

Rachel Otis
@somewhere_under_the_rainbow

Every piece of clothing I choose to adorn my body with is an absolute celebration of my relationship with it and my deeply grown sense of self-love. Eclectic, often whimsical, sometimes vintage, and always full of joy; I live for bold colors, mixing as many prints as possible, and unexpected accessory pairings. I love rompers, bodysuits, and bikinis of all kinds. After being able to let go of how others may perceive my body, I dress to make myself happy — commanding attention and demanding respect.

Photographer:
Sada Reed

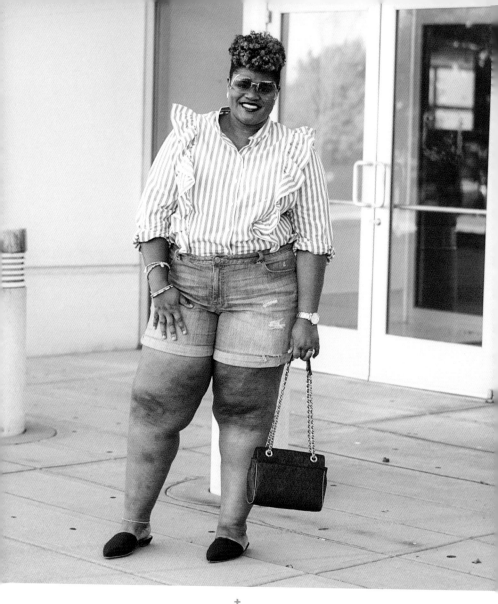

Ashley Carter www.fabellis.com

My style is a mix of classic and vintage.
I love taking great, classic pieces and adding funky vintage
items like kimonos, dresses or accessories.

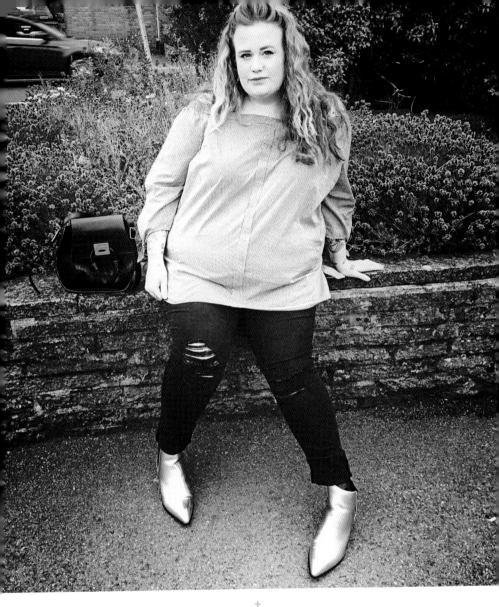

Kate Harding @MrsKateHarding

For me, style is all about being true to yourself. If you want to wear a crop top, wear it, if you want to wear a short skirt or a fitted dress, you wear it. There is nothing worse than desperately wishing you could dress a certain way — I promise you, whatever that way is, you can.

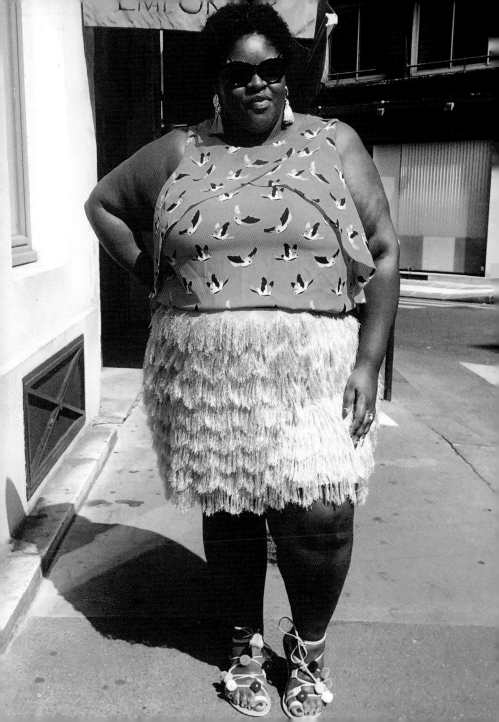

Paty Brown
@Patylicious_Diary

My style is very versatile. I love colors and special fabrics like silk, leather, feathers, glitter, sequins — anything that makes me look different and feel special. I would say I'm in the middle between extravagance and minimalism. For example, I would be crazy in love with an electric blue blazer with big shoulders from the '80s. I remember when I was watching Sex & the City *in the very beginning, I was always obsessed with Samantha, Carrie and Miranda's outfits.*

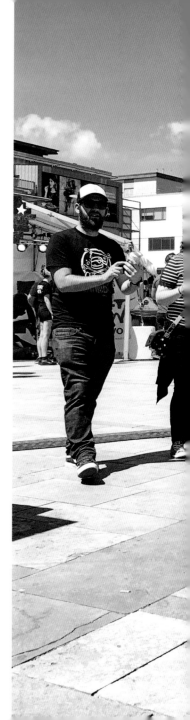

+
Naomi Griffiths
@Naomi_G

I always say my style is "girly tomboy with a hint of glam." I can go from loving and rocking a vintage '50s-inspired dress to ripped jeans, trainers and street wear. I'm hugely inspired by fellow plus-size influencers and love stalking the hashtags on Instagram to see what my next purchase may be!

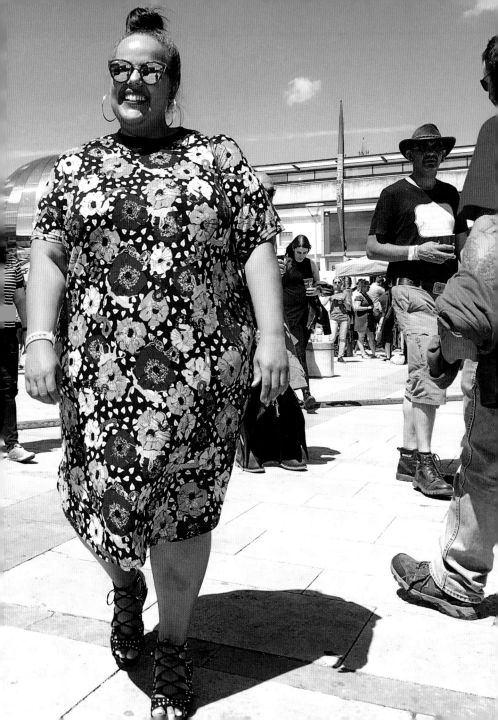

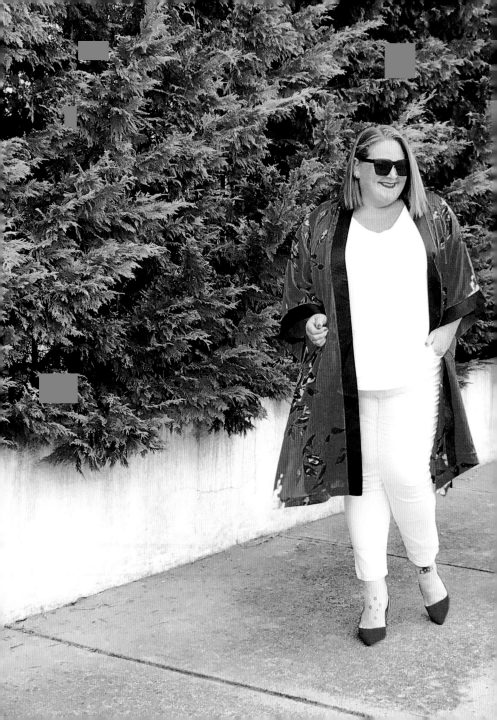

✦

Meghan O'Connor
@littlelimedress

Style is personal and unique to each individual. For me, it's about using fashion as a form of self-expression and a tool to show the world who I am. Confident, chic, polished and playful. My personal style has evolved over the years but there were and are always constants; looking polished and put together effortlessly is key for me. Then, I casually intertwine trend on a practical, wearable level.

Sarah Anne
@Tonsablush

My style changes drastically with my mood. I could be an ultra-sweet schoolgirl one moment and a sultry 1950s pinup the next.

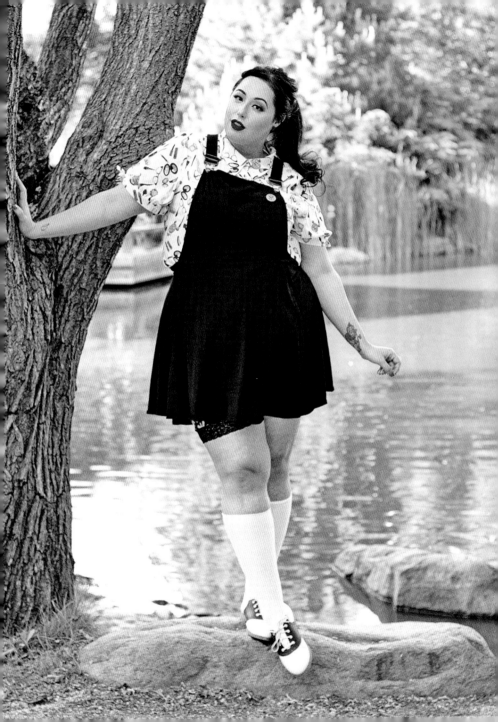

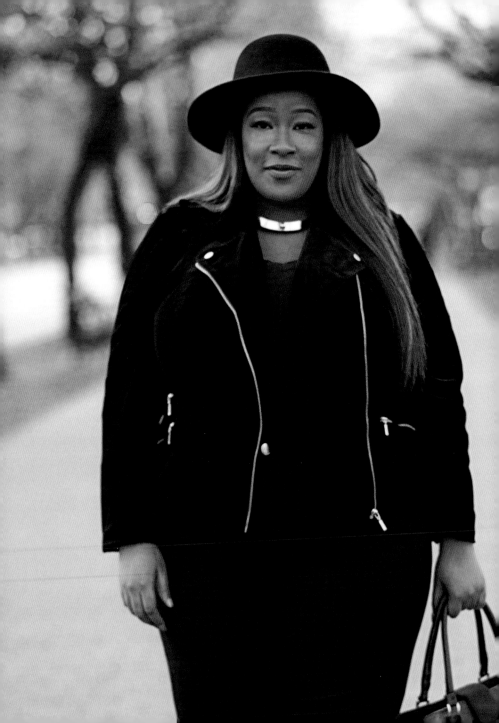

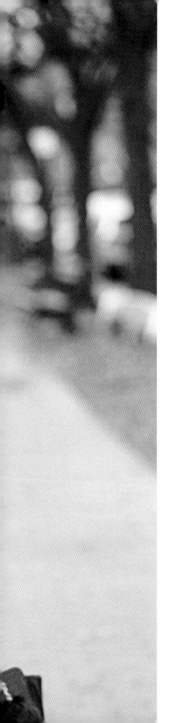

+
Essie Golden
@essiegolden

*I would say my personal style is
described as street, sweet and chic.
I love dresses with sneakers,
a fun bodycon with heels or a bad-
ass trench coat, jeans and hat.
I dress according to my mood
and comfort. I love to try new
things and I'm inspired by the
women of NYC.*

Paulina Luczyk
@For_Fats_Sake

I love playing with vibrant, bright colors and bold patterns and all things that dazzle and sparkle. It's all about the '80s for me — it doesn't really get bolder and brighter than the '80s so obviously that's where I get most of my inspiration from. Blue eye shadow, side ponytails, huge chunky earrings, shoulder pads? Yes please!

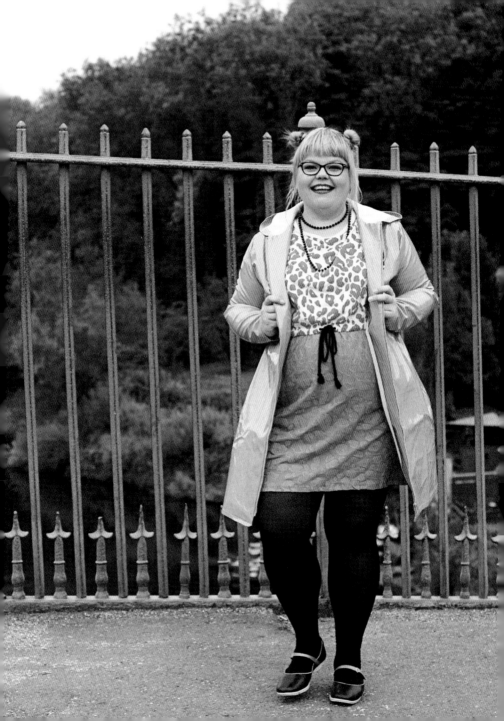

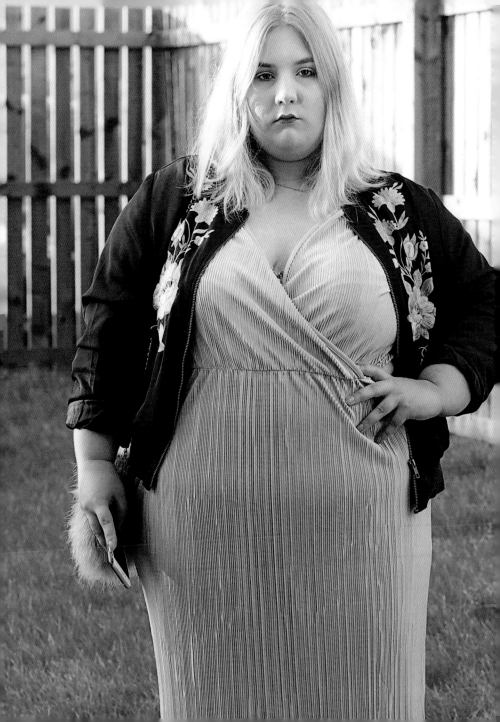

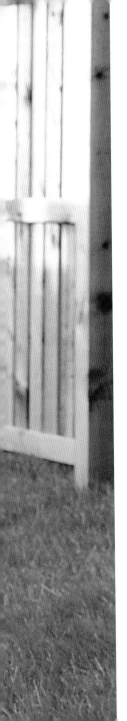

Sarah Moffat
@VelveteenFemme

Just over two years ago I read Marie Kondo's The Life-Changing Magic of Tidying Up *and became instantly obsessed with her philosophy that all possessions should bring you joy. Up to that point, getting dressed had been about compromise and disappointment, but now every piece in my wardrobe — from palm print pajamas to skintight black jeans and pink velvet heels — fills me with a deep, deep joy.*

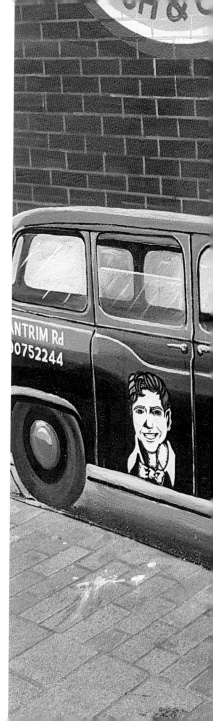

Taylor-Jayne Tytler
@By_TaylorJayne

It has been through discovering babes on Instagram in the last few years that I can say I really came into my own with my personal style. I also moved into working in plus-size retail and I really have found it has helped me become more confident. I decided that my only style goal is to be happy in it myself whether it is in an all-black OOTD or an '80s reject OOTD. I am happy in my skin so I am happy in my clothes.

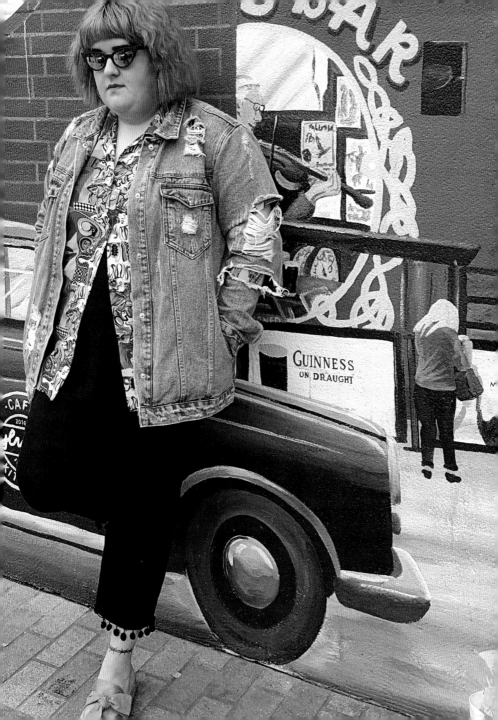

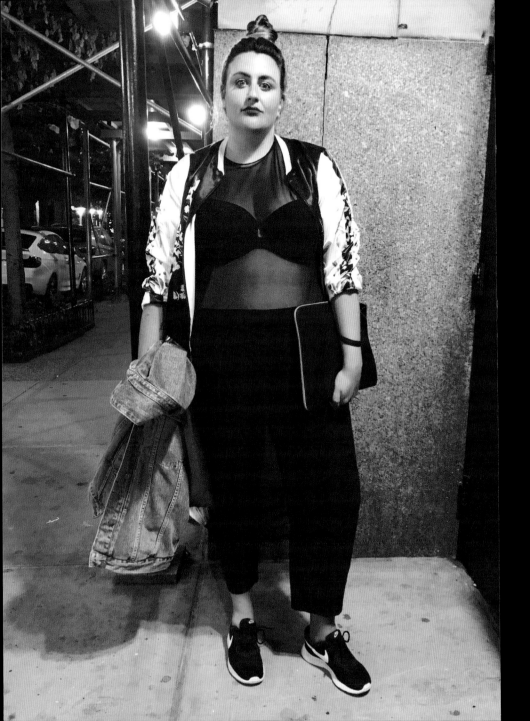

Amanda Richards
@AmandaKater

I usually describe my style as minimalist and as chic as possible — I really enjoy looking expensive despite the fact that I am broke at most times. However, I leave room for my style to go off the rails every once in a while — a loud print, a mesh dress, something with sequins. I like having classic standby pieces that I know I love (yes, mostly in black) but also random, totally non-cohesive stuff that I can wear when I'm feeling like a different version of myself.

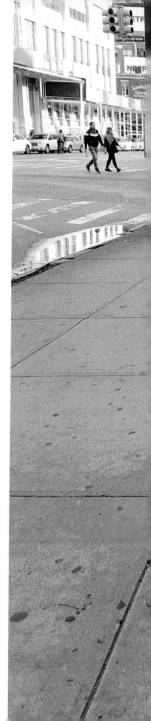

+

Nicole Rieder

@TheHeftyHideaway

My style is inspired a great deal by women, music, and pop culture I am obsessed with. So much of it is throwback '50s, '60s, and '70s style with a modern twist. I often feel as though I was born too late; like imagine being at Whisky a Go-Go in the '60s or CBGB in the '70s — MY GOSH! I am always thrifting and seeking out the best vintage items in my size, which is like looking for a diamond in the rough, to be quite frank.

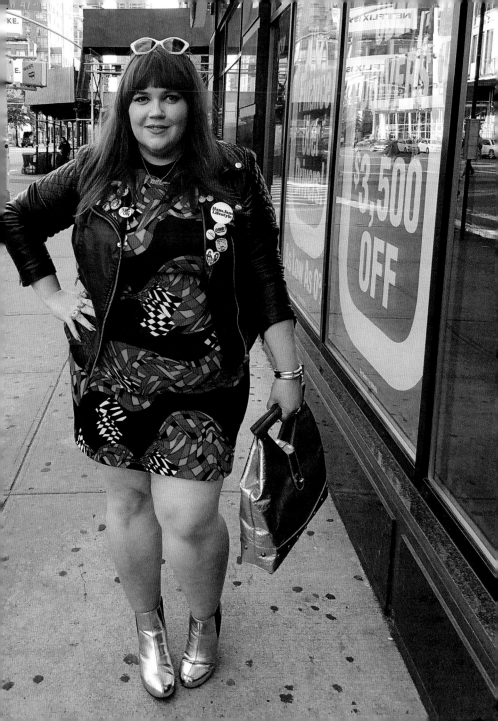

+ I find my

in daring to

fat and

anarchy
be
fashionable.+

—Lottie Moor

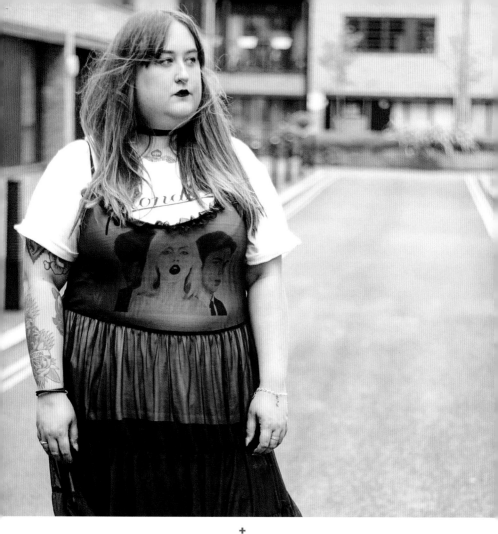

+

Lottie Moor @LottieLamour

It's important for my style to reflect who I am. I am feminine, I am rebellious and I am proud of who I am and where I've come from. This look is the epitome of all of those things.
Photographer: Emma Gunn

+

Mayah Thomas @mayah.camara

To sum up my style I would say "expressive." I believe that fashion is a form of expression and I like to dress to my mood. My wardrobe has everything from puffy swing dresses, skin-tight pleather, sassy lace, sumptuous velvet, denims, sequins . . . you name it I have it!

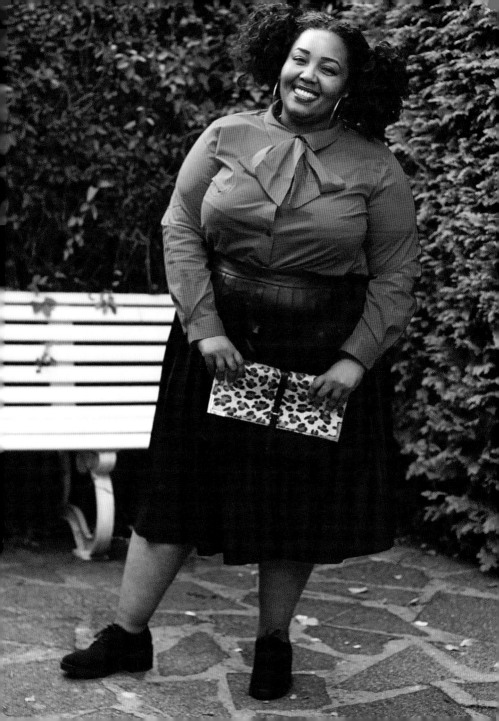

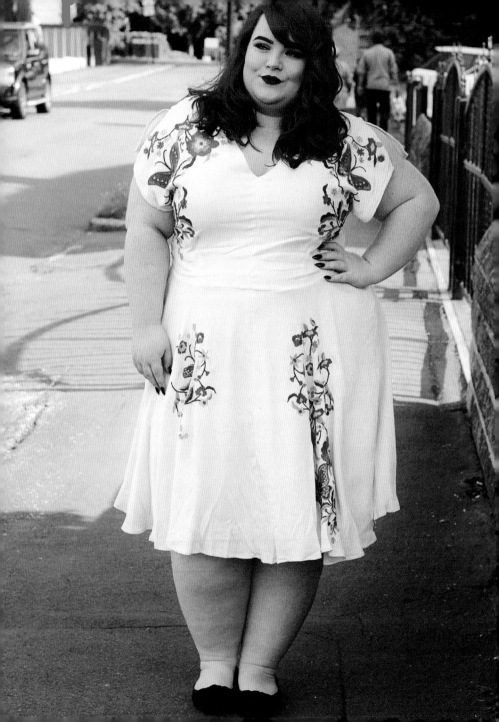

Georgina Grogan
@GeorginaGrogan_

I'm lucky that I get to try many different styles and fashions but I keep coming back to modern vintage — that's the style I feel suits me best and I feel most confident in. Vintage-looking with a twenty-first-century twist.

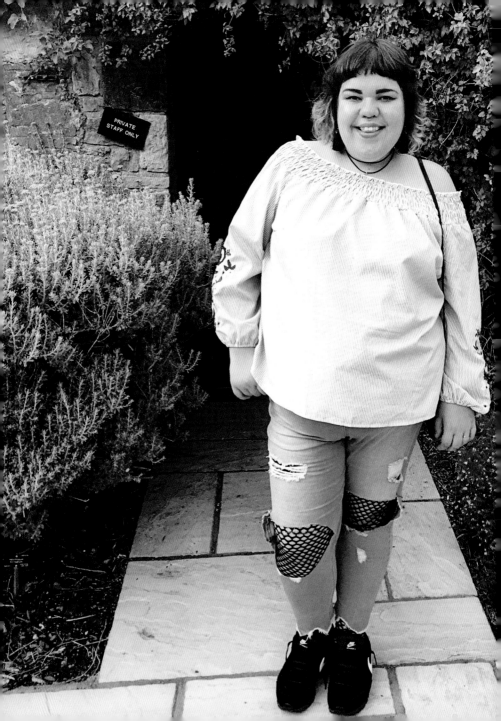

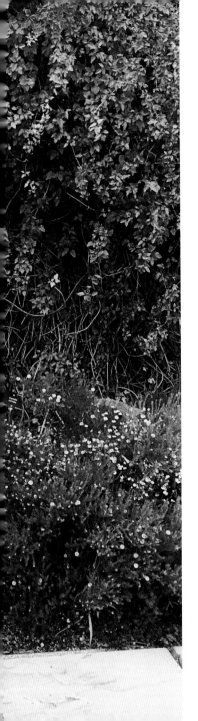

Melanie Chillag
@MellyMeep

I would describe my style as "futch fatty." I really want to reject the notion that fat women must present inherently feminine. I much prefer minimal, sporty, tailored.

Natalie Johnson
@hentai.hunny

My style has always been a constant journey, I love discovering new trends and challenging them with my own personal style. Fashion is something I've always loved and I'd never deprive myself of because of my body. If anything, my size plays a major role in my style and passion.

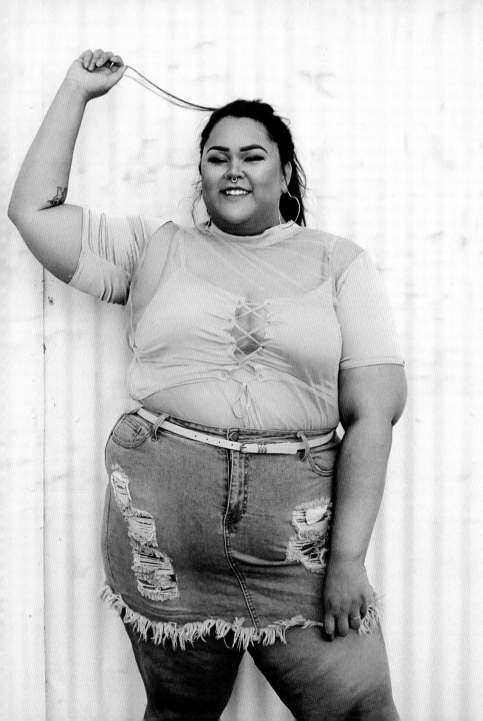

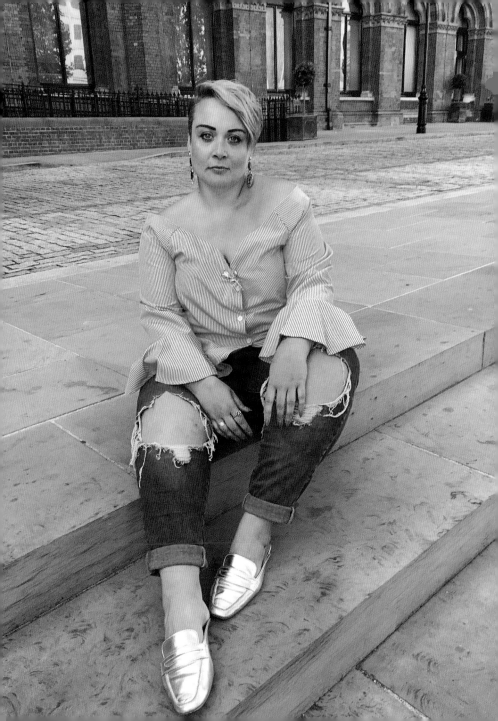

Becky Barnes
@BeckyBarnesBlog

As I've gotten older my style has evolved into slightly more fuss free and comfortable but hopefully still bold enough to make a statement.

✦
Sarah Chiwaya
@Curvily

*My style is a bit eclectic, as for
me fashion is a tool to use to
express who I want to be on any
given day. I lean toward clean
minimal pieces some days, and
sometimes I want to go over the
top with color and print. All
in all, my style complements my
home of NYC: multifaceted, full
of surprises, and a bit edgy.*

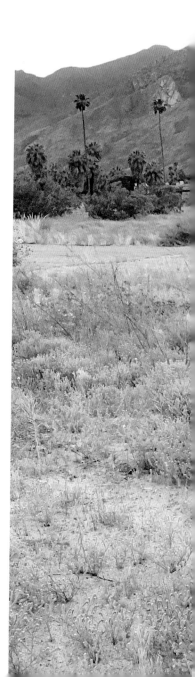

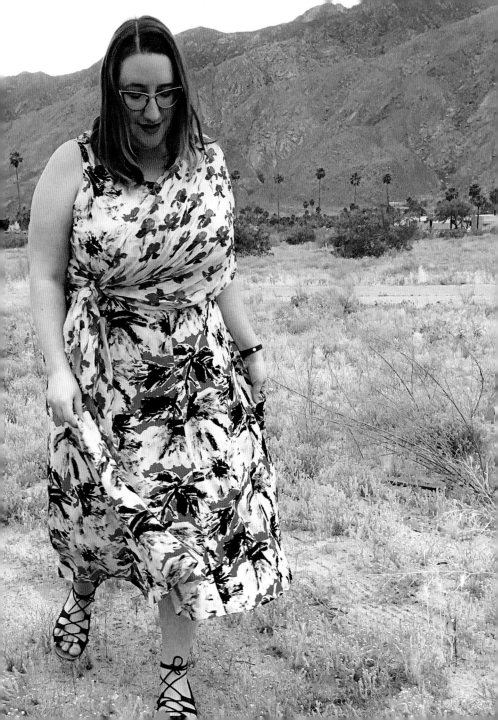

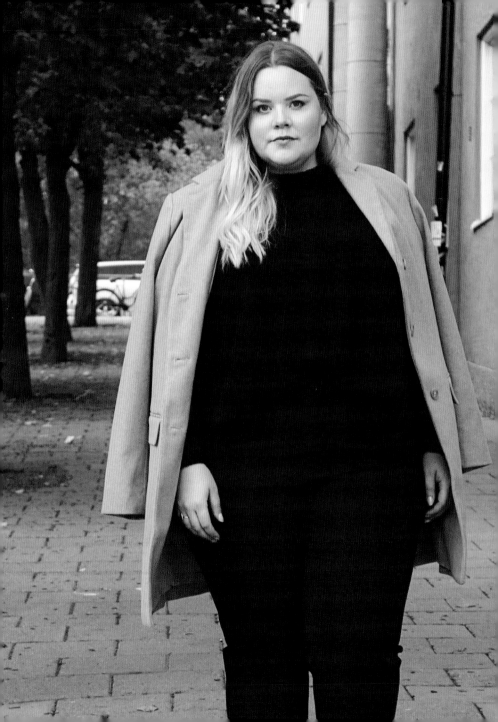

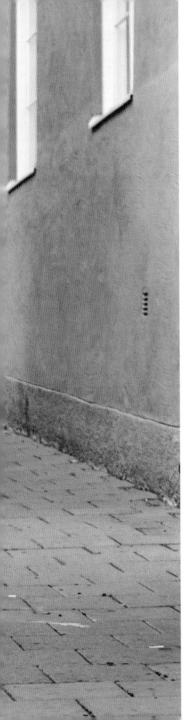

+

Emmi Snicker
@EmmiSnicker

*I would describe my style
as minimalistic and typical
Scandinavian with basic colors
and pieces in the closet.
I love quality garments
and like less is more when
it comes to styling.*

Jessica Hinkle
@ProudMaryFashion

Fashion was the first way I expressed a growing love for my body and shedding of self-hate that was taught to me for so long by the media and society. The fashion world has notoriously been unwelcoming to fat people and has all these "rules" to keep it exclusionary. I don't like to follow those rules. I much prefer to treat style like a form of wearable art. I adorn my body with what I want when I want. And I encourage others to do the same!

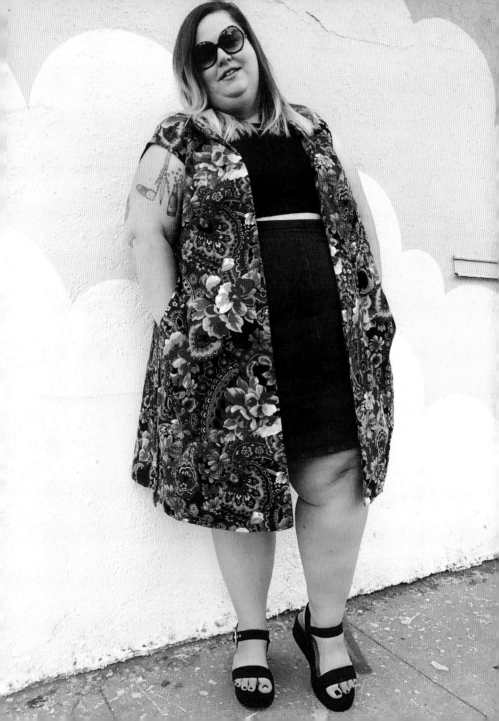

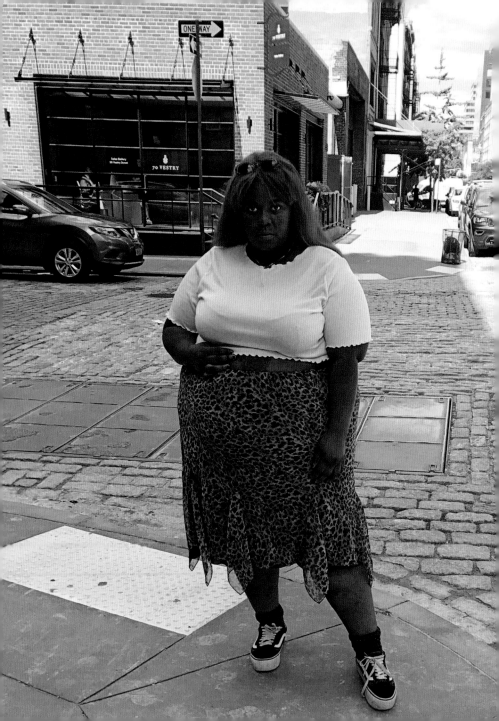

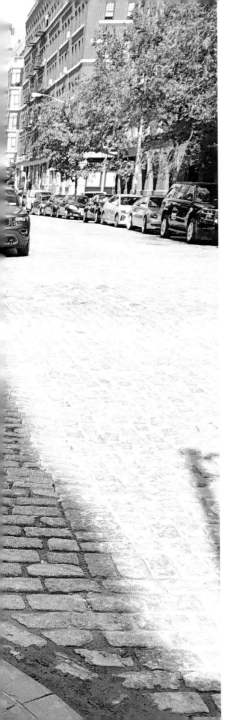

+

La'shaunae Steward
@Luhshawnay

*My style is a mixture of the
early 2000s and the '90s, I love
primary colors and I love mixing
patterns and different fabrics.
My style inspos are Bratz dolls,
Leigh Bowery, Rihanna, Brooke
Candy, and Tyler the Creator.
My style is all about not only
owning my size, but proving to
people that just because you are
a certain size doesn't mean you
can't wear amazing things.
Literally own it!*

LuAnne D'Souza
@WeeshasWorld

My style tends to be influenced by my mood for the day, I never plan outfits and love the creative process of putting pieces together to reflect how I feel. Being body positive, I try to make a conscious decision to get out of my comfort zone and wear things that scare me — like these dungarees! They're not the most flattering on me but who cares — I like it, so I wear it.

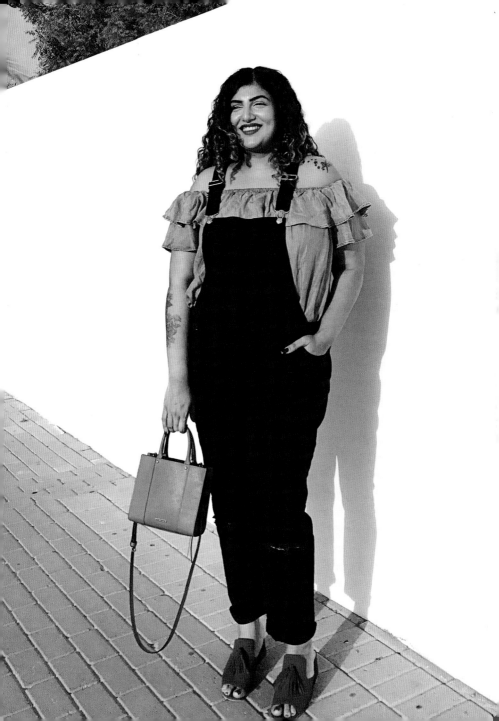

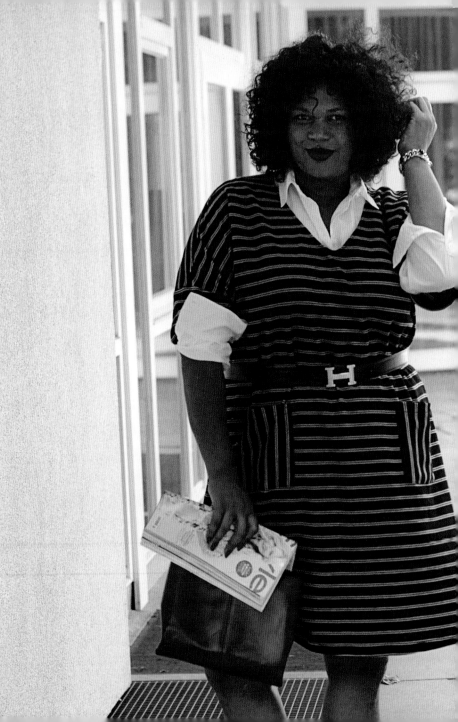

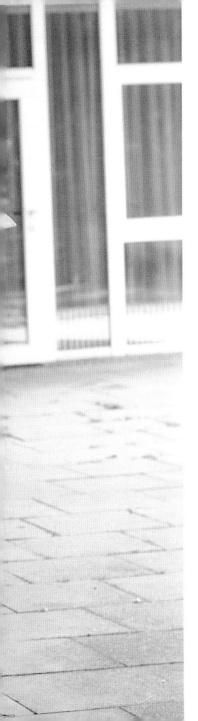

+
Christine Chlench
@Chlencherei

My mum was, and still is, my style role model. She was a very classy lady! So, I would describe my style as classic and clean — with a twist.

Photographer:
Dirk Chlench

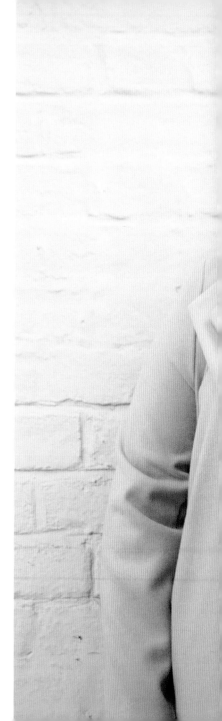

Callie Thorpe
@CallieThorpe

I like to incorporate trends into my looks each season but I always have my go-to items: a moto jacket, a simple jumpsuit and a bold, bright lip.

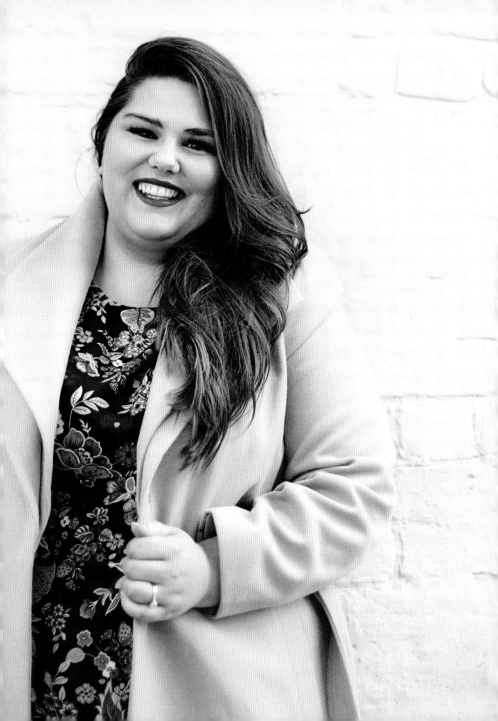

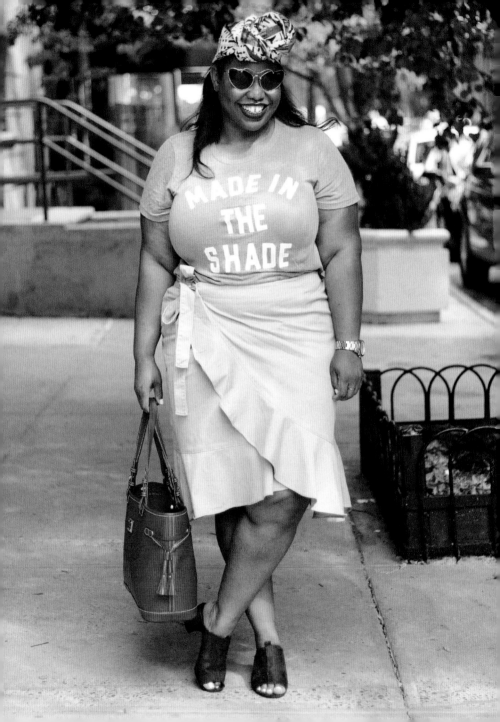

Jamilyn Griggs
@styleoversize

I would say that my style is a juxtaposition of styles. I would wear a classic like the wrap skirt, but with an update like a ruffle. There's a hint of classic in what I wear, but it is always a little something extra to make it special.

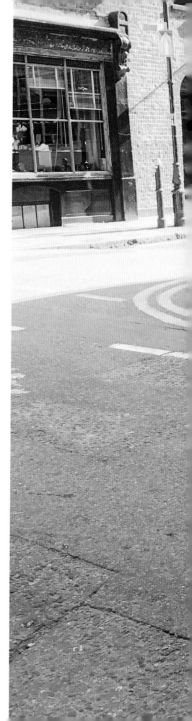

+

Lauren Smeets
@Curvy_Roamer

*Always hard to sum up my style,
but honestly I'd say . . . eclectic —
I don't like to limit myself to one
particular look. One day I'll dress
like a skater boy; Converse, baggy
jeans and a bomber and the
next day I'll go for "bougie and
fabulous" — big earrings, even
bigger hair and a leopard print
dress. Basically wearing whatever
I bloody like since '89, and not
letting my size hinder that.*

Photographer:
Tiffany Baron

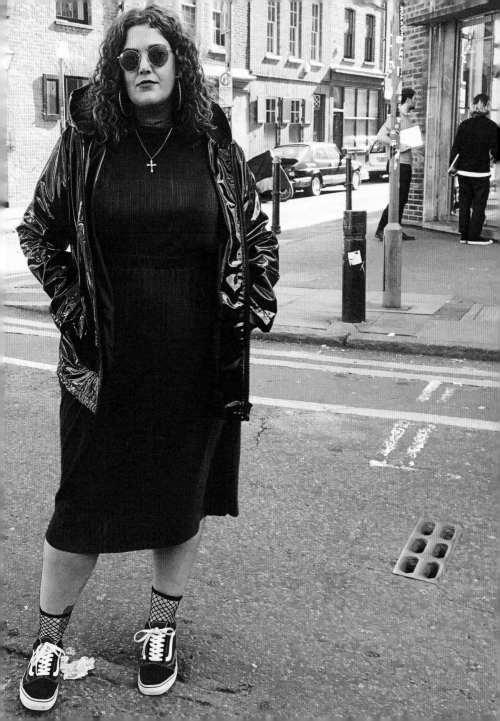

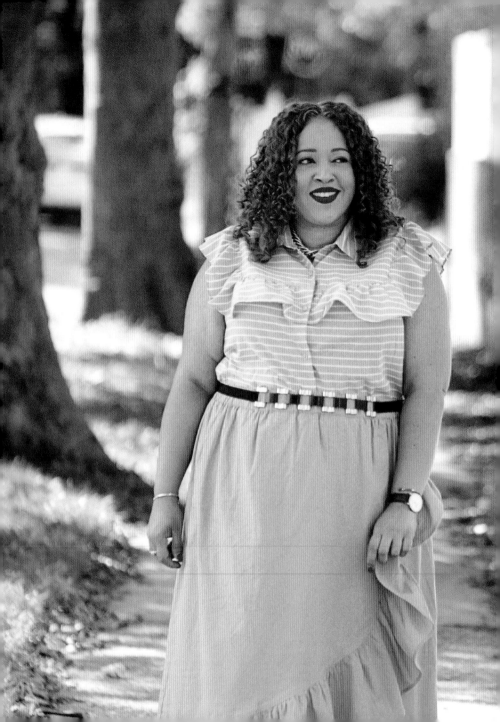

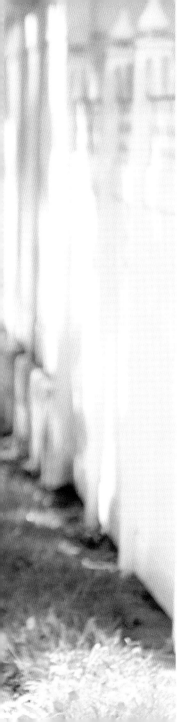

✦

Sandra Negron
@LaPecosaPreciosa

*I consider my style super feminine
and girly, with a sophisticated
flair and a touch of chic.*

Michaela Gingell
@mckayla

I love to look for up-and-coming fashion trends and add a quirky fun twist to it to make it my own. I wear what I want and avoid all these so-called do's and don'ts. Fashion for me is all about having fun and your personality shining through which I always try to achieve with each look.

Photographer: Lauren French

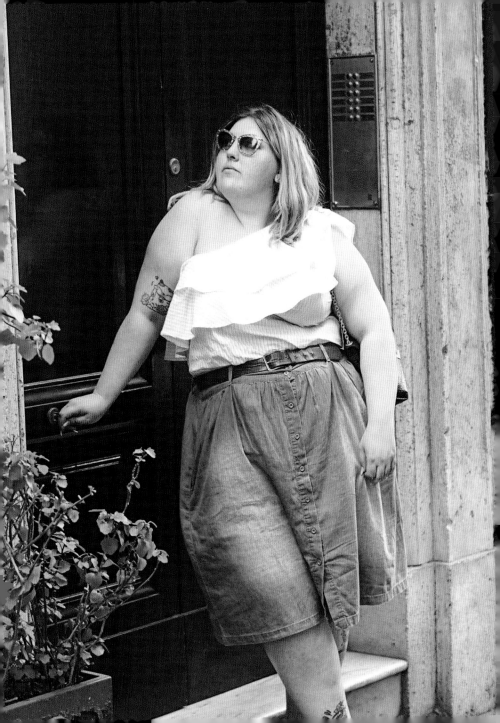

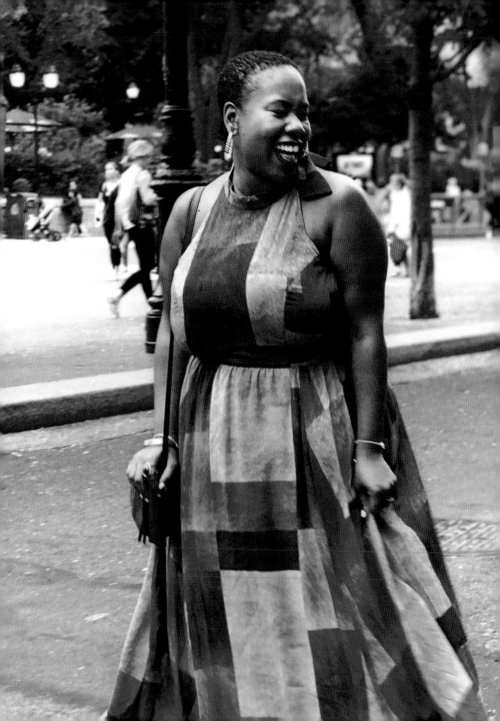

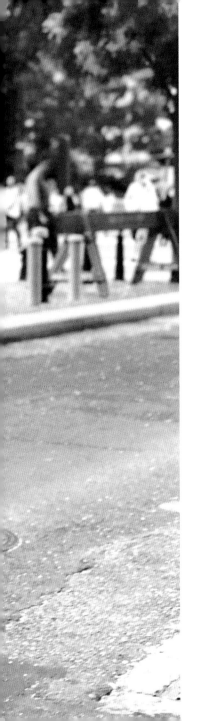

+

Kelly Augustine @
KellyAugustineB

*My personal style is a true
reflection of how I'm feeling
at any given moment. During
the summer, I'm usually more
feminine and fancy-free and in
the colder months I'm a lot
more edgy. Through it all,
I like to keep it very classic and
minimal, yet fun and interesting.*

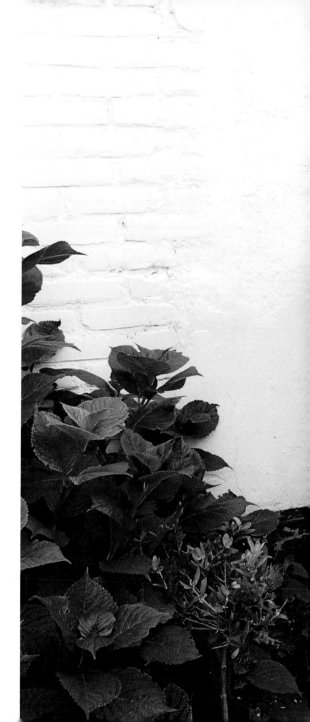

Josine Wille
@TheBiggerBlog

A new day, a new style! I consider each day to be an excuse to wear something different. Preppy and girly is what I love, but some days it's casual all the way.

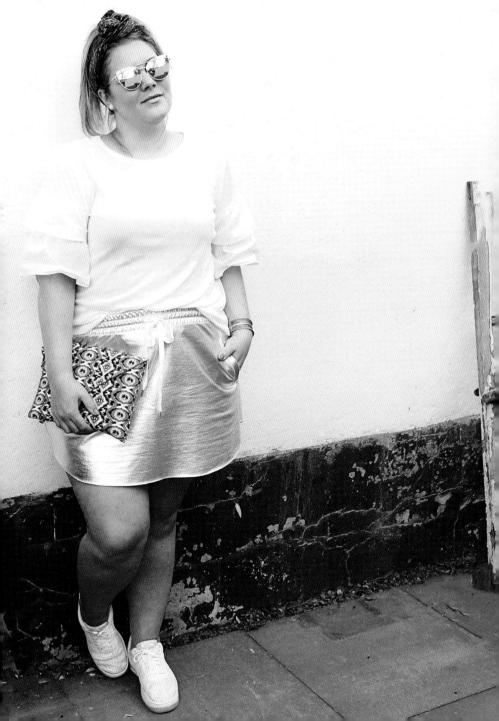

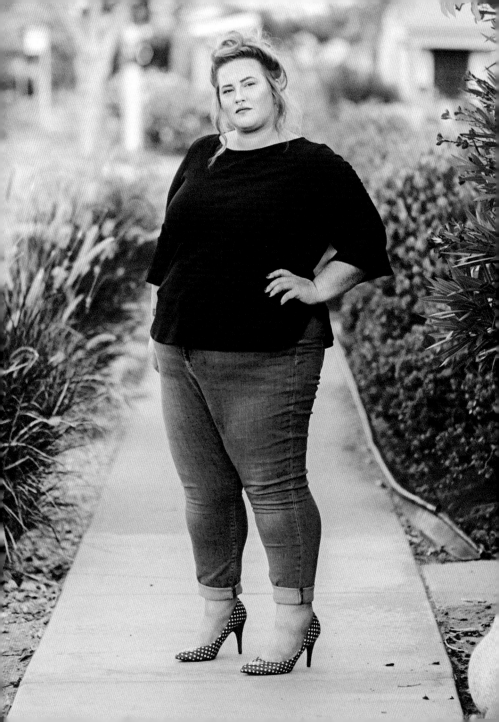

Jessy Parr
@modachrome

I tend to err on the minimalist side of fashion. To me, there's something really classic about a neutral palette with a single statement piece or pop of color. Don't let your clothing wear you, but allow your favorite pieces to speak for themselves and reflect who you are.

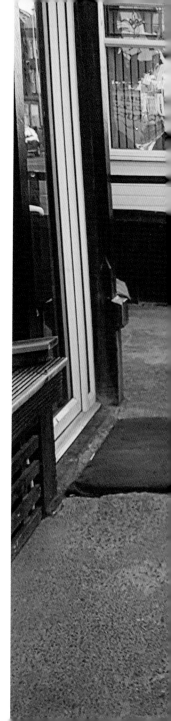

✛
Deborah Aiken
@WannabePrincessUK

At the upper-end of plus-size fashion, I love to break fashion rules — but I also love to be comfortable. I'm most often seen in pretty dresses — with bright patterns and colorful prints.
I never shy away from color and unusual prints like this one are my favorite. I also love an excuse to get my arms or legs out, which pretty skater-style dresses help me do perfectly.

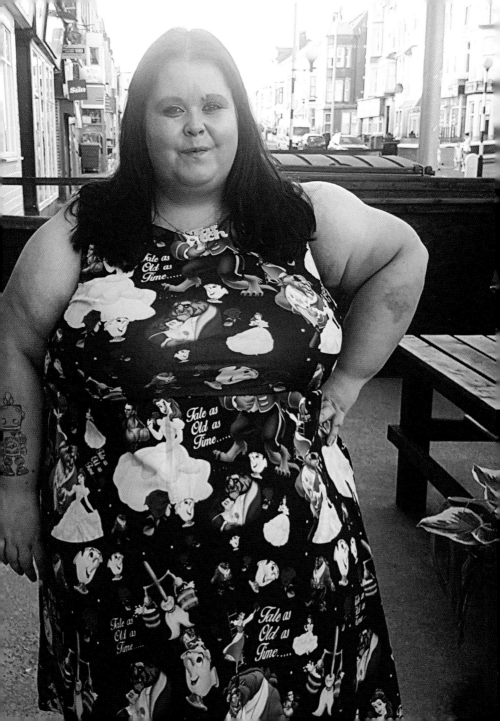

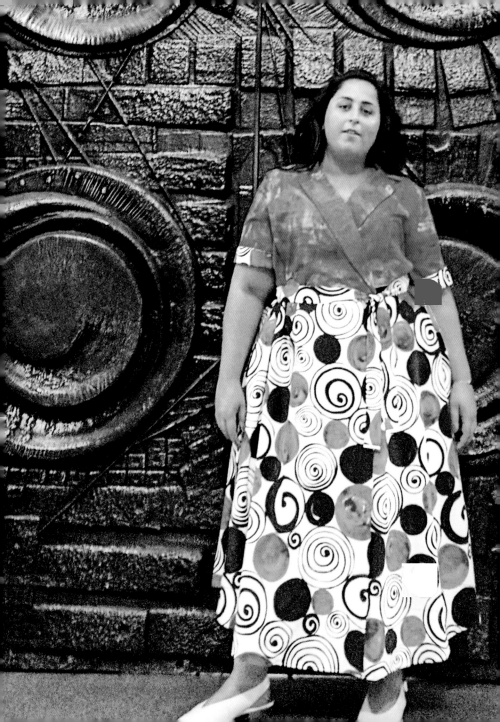

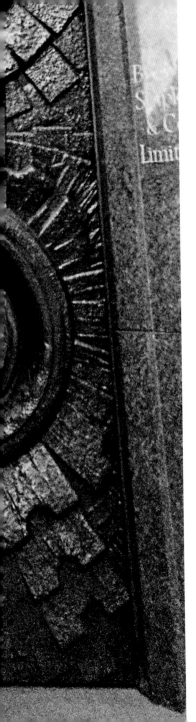

Maryam Pasha
@MaryamPasha

*My style is heavily influenced by
my mood. You are as likely to
see me in all black as you are in
colors and patterns. Regardless
I feel most myself when I'm put
together and comfortable —
I live in flats! My look needs to
make a statement, with high-
quality fabrics and distinct
detail without being fussy or
high maintenance.*

Leah Vernon
@LVernon2000

My personal style is very hard to describe. I'd say it's non-trendy. I don't read fashion magazines because all that stuff is trendy and in. I like street and I like glamour.

Photographer: Michael Chapman

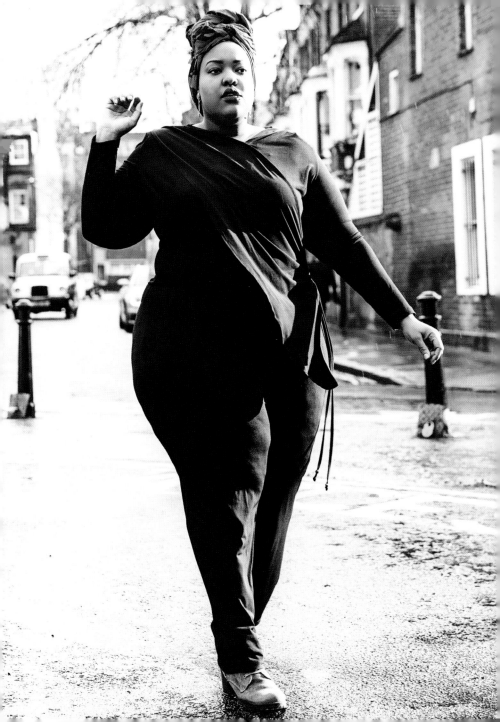